JOURNAL *of a* LONELY GOD

The book of Genesis
reveals God's deepest longing—*You!*

Mike Tucker

Pacific Press® Publishing Association
Nampa, Idaho
Oshawa, Ontario, Canada

www.pacificpress.com

Designed by Eucaris L. Galicia
Cover photo © Robert Meyer/GoodSalt.com

Additional copies of this book are available by calling toll-free 1-800-765-6955
or by visiting www.adventistbookcenter.com

ISBN: 0-8163-2071-3

05 06 07 08 09 · 5 4 3 2 1

CONTENTS

INTRODUCTION

A lonely God? What pictures come to mind when you think of the possibility of God actually being lonely? Do you see Him as weak, needy, or depressed? Does He seem less like a real God? That's not what comes to my mind. It doesn't bother me to think of God as being lonely. In fact, it bothers me to think that God is never lonely—that He never feels what I feel. I find comfort in the picture of God summarized by mid-twentieth-century author and pastor A. W. Tozer: "In the deep of His mighty nature He thinks, wills, enjoys, feels, loves, desires, and suffers as any other person may."

Scripture seems to indicate that our God is a God of strong emotion. The author of Hebrews wrote: "For we do not have a high priest who is unable to sympathize with our weaknesses, but we have one who has been tempted in every way, just as we are—yet was without sin. Let us then approach the throne of grace with confidence, so that we may receive mercy and find grace to help us in our time of need" (Hebrews 4:15, 16).

Countless other texts tell us of God feeling anger, sorrow, regret, love, and great joy. The Bible paints God's portrait in colors that convey strong emotions, strong desires.

Could it be that God has unmet longings? Is it possible that God has a desire for a deeper relationship with you that is yet unfulfilled?

I am drawn to the picture of a God of passion. I am drawn to a God who longs for me and promises to create in me a longing for intimacy with Him.

It occurs to me that much of the Bible is the story of God's longing. It is the story of His desire for intimacy—for a close relationship with beings who can choose to love Him, and therefore, choose to reject Him.

Why else would a God who knows the beginning from the end choose to create beings He knows will ultimately reject Him? Why else would He work with the Son and the Holy Spirit to devise a plan to rescue those whose sin has sentenced them to eternal death? Why else would He put Himself through all that trouble—all that sacrifice, all that pain and heartbreak?

There can be only one reason. Ours is a God who, more than anything else, longs for fellowship. He longs for close relationships with those who choose to love Him. So great is this longing that He has chosen to take any risk, experience any pain, and suffer any rejection necessary to arrive at His ultimate desire—intimate, unbroken fellowship with you!

This is how I see most of Scripture. The Bible is chiefly a book of stories. The gospel comes to us as story. God reveals Himself to us as story. And the gist of the story is this: God loves you too much to let anything stand in the way of uninterrupted fellowship with you!

This is especially true of the book of Genesis. The stories of God's dealings with Adam, Abraham, and Isaac are the stories of God reaching out to His creation with an invitation to fellowship. When you read them, it's almost as if you are looking over God's shoulder and peeking at entries in His journal—the journal of a lonely God.

One thing to remember though: God does not react to loneliness as you and I might. When God is lonely, He creates a world! When that world rejects Him, He provides a costly redemption. And when it seems that nobody understands Him, He searches out individuals with the potential for friendship and makes Himself more deeply known. He offers Himself to them in various ways—over and over. He promises to forgive their failures, heal their wounds, fulfill their longings, and eventually take them to a place of uninterrupted, eternal fellowship.

Perhaps the most surprising thing my study of Genesis has revealed to me is that God is actually lonely for me! As feeble and sinful as I am, God still is lonely for me! And the more I think about that, the more the thought makes me lonely for Him as well. How about you?

Join me as we read from God's Genesis journal. Experience the longings of His great heart for you, and see if it doesn't awaken in you a longing for Him as well!

Mike Tucker

Creation

GENESIS 1–2

After decades of studying human nature, the great psychoanalyst and writer Viktor Frankl came to this conclusion: Life boils down to one thing—the search for meaning. That's what we're all really pursuing. All other questions are secondary.

What's the purpose of my life? Why am I here? An awful lot of people have no clue.

Lee Iacocca, in his book *Straight Talk*, wrote, "Here I am in the twilight years of my life, still wondering what it's all about. . . . I can tell you this, fame and fortune is for the birds."

What's it all about? Why am I alive?

I believe the best answer to these essential questions is found back at the beginning. There are important clues in the *genesis* of life. Learning how we got here can help us understand our meaning.

Some scientists seem certain we are here by chance. They tell us that our existence is a great cosmic accident. A galactic explosion at just the right time, when all the right chemicals just happened to be present in precisely the right amounts, somehow produced the spark that set life ablaze, that created that first single cell. And many scientists still try to believe that this cell somehow evolved into more cells, and that the incredibly complex DNA language of life was written all by random processes, all by chance.

I believe that the Old Testament book of Genesis gives us a starting point that makes a lot more sense. It's an account of origins that explains why we are all driven by this search for meaning. Genesis means "beginnings." It's the earliest written record of the history of God's interaction with human beings. Moses, the book's likely author, could not borrow from other printed material.

There are two probable sources for Moses' information. First, there existed a great oral tradition. In ancient times before written histories developed, people told stories from one generation to another. Those stories created an important oral history and were the only link many generations had to the past. It's possible that Moses got some of his information from this oral tradition.

However, Moses' main exposure to this tradition had to have come during his first twelve years of life. That's the period when his mother served as his nanny for Pharaoh's daughter. He could have heard stories about Creation from her. But it is more likely that much of Moses' detailed information came directly from Someone else, directly from God. The stories of Genesis themselves seem to call for a divine source.

Genesis is primarily a storybook—a collection of stories given by God to Moses. Much of what we know of God during Old Testament times comes to us in the form of story. That's the medium God chose for the transmission of His good news. The stories in Genesis focus on God's desire for relationship with human beings from the very beginning, from our planet's birth. There is a sense in which Genesis is the journal of God the Creator, a journal He passed on to Moses.

And as we read Genesis, we discover that it is the journal of a lonely God. God longed for fellowship, so He created man. When man broke that fellowship through disobedience, God provided a means of reconciliation. He wanted man back. And the way human beings could experience that reconciliation was through a particular relationship, a relationship with God's Son, Jesus.

The rest of the Bible is the story of how God pursued man in an effort to be known by him and to be loved by him. It is the incredible story of an infinite, perfect God's longing for imperfect human beings, the story of His intense desire for every generation to know Him and to love Him.

That's the essence of Genesis. It is the journal of a lonely God.

God begins His journal in a simple, straightforward fashion. He gives no background or explanation; He simply states: "In the beginning God created the heavens and the earth" (Genesis 1:1).

Intellectuals have questioned this bold claim for a century and a half. In fact, in some academic circles, you are definitely out of step if you are so naïve as to believe that God created the heavens and the earth. But many other scientists today have been driven by the evidence to believe there had to be a designer; life couldn't possibly have come about by chance.

Let me give you an example. Patrick Glynn is a professor, educated at Harvard and Oxford, and a research specialist at George Washington University. He's written a book titled *God, The Evidence: The Reconciliation of Faith and Reason in a Postsecular World*. In this book, Glynn sites a presentation made in 1973 to the International Astronomical Union by Brandon Carter, a physicist and cosmologist.

Dr. Carter called attention to what he called the anthropic principle. This principle amounts to a refutation of the original premise behind the idea of a random universe. Carter pointed out that life had to be preplanned from the very origin of the cosmos. He said that if life was to appear in the universe, everything had to be just right from the very first nanosecond the universe came into being.

Glynn, while discussing Carter's theory, writes:

> The possibility of producing life depended on everything being "just right" from the very start—everything from the values of fundamental forces like electromagnetism and gravity, to the relative masses of the various subatomic particles, to things like the number of neutrino types. . . . The slightest tinkering with a single one of scores of basic values and relationships in nature would have resulted in a universe very different from the one we inhabit—say, one with no stars like our sun, or no stars, period. Far from being accidental, life appeared to be the goal toward which the entire universe from the very first moment of its existence had been orchestrated, fine-tuned (pp. 7, 8).

Glynn and Carter, and many other scientists, have concluded that it certainly appears someone had to decide long beforehand exactly how things would work, exactly how life would turn out. It had to be planned long before the first living cell started reproducing.

Physicists are also joining in this chorus. They've long wondered why the values of what are called fundamental constants are set as they are. Why was the gravitational force or the electromagnetic force set a certain way? Why not different values?

As it turns out, if these values varied ever so slightly, life in our universe would be impossible. Scores of fundamental constants have to be exactly right or everything falls apart. So when you do the math, when you look at the numbers, it gets harder and harder to talk about accidents and blind chance.

Carter's anthropic principle declares that a common thread runs through all the fundamental constant values of the universe. Glynn puts it this way: "The anthropic principle says that all the seemingly arbitrary and unrelated constants in physics have one strange thing in common—these are precisely the values you need if you want to have a universe capable of producing life" (p. 22).

Carter argues that it's hard to escape the conclusion that the universe has a purpose, that it's made a certain way in order to ultimately result in the creation of human life. All the other processes in the universe are aimed in that direction. Everything seems designed toward that end.

Glynn gives a few interesting examples. If gravity were slightly weaker than it is, our sun could not support human life. If the "nuclear weak force" had been slightly weaker, all the hydrogen in the universe would have been turned to helium, and there would be no water anywhere. A "nuclear strong force" just 2 percent stronger than it is would have prevented the formation of protons—there would be no atoms in the universe. Even the nature of something as common as water is no accident. It doesn't behave according to the standard laws of chemistry. It's not heavier as a solid than as a liquid. And there's an important reason for that. If frozen water, ice, were heavier than unfrozen water, the oceans and rivers would freeze from the bottom up, and all living things in them would die.

What we're seeing today is that the latest thinking in science supports the basic ideas of Genesis. The deeper we peer into the structure of the universe and the structure of atomic particles, the more we see design and purpose; the more we see the hand of a Creator.

Our existence is not some cosmic accident. It's the intentional act of a God who was lonely. There is marvelous evidence of a Master Designer creating a terribly complex universe. There is great scientific support for the theory of special creation as presented in Scripture.

But now let's turn to something more specific. Let's look at some evidence from science that fills in the picture of our Creator a bit. It tells us something about His nature and His love for each one of us.

The anthropic principle nails down the fact that a great deal of complicated scientific data all work together precisely to make a certain kind of life possible. And that suggests that someone went to an awful lot of trouble. Someone invested a great deal of intelligence and ingenuity and creativity. It suggests, in other words, that God had a plan, a precisely developed plan, for creating a life form that was capable of intimacy with Him. After all, we now know that the slightest variation in "fundamental constants" would erase the possibility that you and I exist as conscious beings. Everything in the universe is designed to sustain a particular kind of life, and it's the kind of life that can enjoy fellowship with its Creator. God created the universe with you in mind.

"In the beginning God created the heavens and the earth." Before time began, God planned for you. He longed to know you and to be known by you, so He prepared a place for you.

Genesis tells us that after God created the universe—after He hung the stars and planets in space, after He covered the land with flora and fauna, after He filled the seas with living things, after all that—He created man. It was only after the setting was complete that He turned His attention to the crowning act of creation. And God made an actual companion for Himself. He made someone to share the beauties of nature with. He made someone to know and love. He made someone who could know and love Him.

That is how we got here. And that is the ultimate purpose of human beings. We were created for the purpose of knowing and loving God. We were created for fellowship with God.

That purpose is stamped on our very bodies. Sir Isaac Newton said, "In the absence of any other proof, the thumb alone would convince me of God's existence." And what we know today about the human body only confirms this conclusion. For example, the late scientific writer Carl Sagan, an atheist, wrote that a single human chromosome contains "billions and billions" of bits of information. Twenty billion bits, to be exact, the equivalent of about three billion letters, which is equal to about five hundred million words, which would total approximately two million pages, which would fill about four thousand textbooks.

So what should we conclude about that? Well, if a single human chromosome contains an enormous library of information, how can we not conclude that we are exquisitely and intricately designed creatures?

The Bible declares,

> So God created man in his own image,
> in the image of God he created him;
> male and female he created them (Genesis 1:27).

Interestingly enough, God created beings who reminded Him of Himself.

I remember reading a Christmas play that featured a monologue by Joseph, moments after the birth of Jesus. He spoke to the little One in his arms. Looking into the Baby's face, he gushed playfully about how His nose and eyes resembled His mother's. But then he paused and, in all seriousness, whispered, "I wonder what Your Father looks like."

I vividly remember the moments when I looked into the faces of my newborn daughters. I wanted, of course, to find something recognizable, something similar, something of myself in them. I wanted them to look like me. And through the years, people have sometimes told me how my daughters look like their father. That delights me every time. They may not be too thrilled by the idea, but I love the fact that I can see myself in them. They are my daughters, my own flesh and blood.

Now imagine God's feelings as He looked at Adam and Eve, His first human children. I see some loving pride there. I see the smile grow across God's face as He examines those two and sees how they look like their Father. He would never, of course, want to deny they belonged to Him! They were created in His image.

Do you realize that the same holds true for you? Imagine the smile creeping across God's face as He looks at you and sees the ways *you* resemble Him, the ways you reflect that divine image. God would never, ever deny that you belong to Him. You look like your Father! You bear aspects of His image in your appearance and personality and character. And you were designed with the capacity for fellowship, for intimacy, with your Father. That's your purpose. That's your destiny. That's your design. You will never be whole, you will never find life's meaning, until you fulfill this purpose for which you were created.

God was lonely at creation, lonely in the sense that He longed for people to have fellowship with. Well we are incomplete, too, at creation. We come into this world needing to form a bond with someone, needing to find our roots, needing to establish relationships.

God knew this. That's why He didn't make just one human being to put in Eden. "The LORD God said, 'It is not good for the man to be alone. I will make a helper suitable for him' " (Genesis 2:18).

Fellowship. Relationship. That's a hallmark of God's character. He needs to know and to be known—to love and to be loved. And it follows that those who are made in His image naturally have the same needs. We need companionship.

So, God created someone who would complement Adam, someone who would complete him. He made Eve because it was not good for Adam to be alone. It wasn't good for Eve to be alone either.

> So the LORD God caused the man to fall into a deep sleep; and while he was sleeping, he took one of the man's ribs and closed up the place with flesh. Then the LORD God made a woman from the rib he had taken out of the man, and he brought her to the man. The man said,
>
> "This is now bone of my bones
>   and flesh of my flesh;
> she shall be called 'woman,'
>   for she was taken out of man" (Genesis 2:21–23).

God could not have chosen a more intimate way to link the sexes. He formed Eve from Adam's rib. That symbolizes the fact that she was made to stand alongside the man as an equal, as one intended for heart-to-heart fellowship. Man and woman are incomplete without each other. They need fellowship, the fellowship of standing side by side.

But God wasn't finished. He had even more planned for the couple, an even deeper, more intimate relationship. He said, "For this reason a man will leave his father and mother and be united to his wife, and they will become one flesh" (Genesis 2:24).

"One flesh!" What better illustration of intimacy could there be? God wants husbands and wives to enjoy such close intimacy that they feel they're inside each other's skin. It's as if they shared one body. "One flesh!" We were truly created for intimacy; intimacy with God and with each other.

John Guest puts it well: "Just as husband and wife live out their lives against the backdrop of being married, so do we live out the entirety of our lives against the backdrop of a constant relationship with God. He is always there, always loving us, always ready to listen to us. As we recognize His unwavering commitment to us, we are able to live in the day-to-day adventure and challenge of His presence. We enjoy the dialogue. It's as if we say, 'Oh, I must talk to Him about this!' "

My great-grandmother was a simple, uneducated woman who grew up on an Arkansas farm, married a farmer, and raised her daughter on a farm. Toward the end of her life, her mind began to fail. One day her family had to tell her that her husband had died. There was a long silence. Then she remarked, "When we think of something we want to tell him, he won't be there."

I've come to see a good definition of fellowship in those words. Fellowship with God means that whenever anything comes to mind, we share it with Him. After all, the whole of creation is designed to make fellowship possible, fellowship between you and God. When human sin broke that bond, interrupted that fellowship, God came up with a plan to restore it—the plan of redemption. And it was based on fellowship, a relationship with the One who is your Substitute for the penalty of sin. A relationship with Christ is required to restore creation to its original purpose of fellowship with God.

It all comes full circle. Fellowship was at the beginning. Fellowship will be there at the end. Fellowship is the journey. Fellowship is the destination. And we'll be forever incomplete until we join that journey. We'll be incomplete, in other words, until God becomes a friend.

Mary C. Miller has written: "There is within us all a magnetic draw to seek God's presence in a more exclusive way, focusing on divine attention rather than our own egocentric list of do's. If we do not follow that prompting, we end up fragmenting ourselves from our potential as disciples. And we fragment God, expecting the Spirit's love only in spite of ourselves."

We are fragments—pieces separated from their core—as long as we fail to seek God's presence. There is within each of us a great need to fulfill our purpose and become whole through a relationship with God.

Brother Lawrence wrote: "The most holy practice, the nearest to daily life, and the most essential for the spiritual life, is the practice of the presence of God, that is to find joy in his divine company and to make it a habit of life, speaking humbly and conversing lovingly with him at all times, every moment, without rule or restriction, above all at times of temptation, distress, dryness, and revulsion, and even of faithlessness and sin."

God is lonely for you. And whether you realize it or not, you are lonely for God.

Genesis is the journal of that lonely God. It's a journal telling us God was not content to wallow in His loneliness. He decided to do something about it. He created a universe designed to house humanity. He made real relationships possible. And He also created a way to restore broken relationships. Our happiness depends upon our willingness to accept God's offer of restoration and reconciliation.

Thomas Tarrants had dedicated his life to white supremacy. He led Mississippi's White Knights of the Ku Klux Klan, America's most violent right-wing terrorist organization. In the mid-1960s Thomas and his racist buddies waged war on Jews and blacks, especially those speaking out for integration. They bombed synagogues and the homes of NAACP officials.

Captured after a bloody gun battle, Thomas was tried, sentenced, and eventually placed in a maximum security prison. Not unexpectedly, Thomas grew introspective while rotting away in Parchman State Penitentiary. He began actually reading the Bible he had previously used to justify his racism. This time the words of the New Testament about forgiveness, love, and brotherhood sank in. Thomas renounced his right-wing activities as "diametrically opposed" to true Christianity and embraced Christ in faith.

Now this man enjoys a clean slate. People around him sense that his dark past has been blotted out. He has been forgiven and accepted by the Almighty.

Eldridge Cleaver passed through boyhood under an abusive father in the poverty of red-clay Arkansas and then tried to stake out his manhood in a Los Angeles ghetto through rape and drug dealing. Fed up with oppression, like others who became Black Panthers, he decided to hate back. His violent escapades against white racism landed him in jail. After release he got into a shootout with Oakland police and fled the country. But in exile in southern France, the Black Panther found his way to God.

One evening, out on a balcony underneath the star-studded Mediterranean sky, he saw a parade of revolutionary heroes pass before his eyes and quickly drop out of view "like fallen heroes." Then Christ appeared in dazzling light. Cleaver crumbled and wept. He grabbed a Bible his wife had brought along and began reading Psalm 23. A God of mercy seemed to be talking to him loud and clear.

That night he experienced the most peaceful sleep of his life. He later said that when he awoke, "I could see in my mind the way, all the way back home, just as clear as I've ever seen anything."

Forgiven, accepted. The past blotted out.

Talk about southern hospitality! There they stand, Thomas and Eldridge, welcomed home, sipping lemonade on the great broad porch of God's forgiveness, fanning themselves with gentle talk about love and fellowship.

These two characters, nailing down perimeters so far apart, give us a glimpse of the breadth of divine mercy and of the depth of God's longing for us. Most of us would question whether such extremists can really come home. But God just keeps holding the door open on His great broad porch. And He sends out this divine announcement through the prophet Isaiah:

> I revealed myself to those who did not ask for me;
> I was found by those who did not seek me.
> To a nation that did not call on my name,
> I said, "Here am I, here am I" (Isaiah 65:1).

You were intended for fellowship with God. That's why He made you.

That purpose is imprinted in your DNA, in the depths of your soul. And no matter how long the separation, no matter how far you've wandered from your Creator, He remains the lonely God who seeks reconciliation. If we're not with Him, there's always an empty chair at His table.

Real relationships. Genuine intimacy. That's why you're here. What does the Creator of the universe seek from you? Just that you step up on that porch and embrace Him as His child.

2

The Fall From Trust

GENESIS 3

Where do you place your trust?

Have you found something dependable—something solid and time-tested?

Stanley, a homeowner, was getting fed up with crime in the neighborhood. Too many break-ins. Too many prowlers. His suburb just wasn't what it used to be. The city seemed to be getting closer and closer.

So Stanley decided to do something about it. He bought a heavy metal screen door for the front of his house. He had steel bars installed outside all the windows. He put bolts on all the doors. He wired a security system that automatically locked everything up.

Finally Stanley felt safe. Nobody was going to break in to his castle.

But, a few weeks later, a fire started in his kitchen while Stanley was taking a nap. Awakened by the smoke, he tried to rush outside. But all the doors were bolted shut, and all the windows were barred. Sadly, he wasn't able to disarm the locks before succumbing to the fire.

Where do you place your trust? Has it proven to be trustworthy? Are you certain you can trust it with your life?

For decades, anyone living within five or six miles of the factory in Denver, Pennsylvania, set their clocks and watches by the sirens the timekeeper at the factory set off five days a week. Most people began their day when the wake-up siren sounded at 5:30 A.M. That was followed, at designated times without fail, by the starting-time siren, the lunchtime siren, and the quitting-time siren.

One day however, the venerable siren system had to be dismantled. The local paper ran a story on the timekeeper. A reporter asked, "What do you use to determine the exact time?"

With a twinkle in his eye, the man reached in his pocket and pulled out a child's Mickey Mouse watch.

For all those years, the town of Denver, Pennsylvania, had entrusted the keeping of the exact time to—where Mickey's hands pointed!

What do you place your trust in?

The third chapter of the book of Genesis tells us a story of broken trust. This is how the journal of a lonely God relates it:

> Now the serpent was more crafty than any of the wild animals the LORD God had made. He said to the woman, "Did God really say, 'You must not eat from any tree in the garden'?" The woman said to the serpent, "We may eat fruit from the trees in the garden, but God did say, 'You must not eat fruit from the tree that is in the middle of the garden, and you must not touch it, or you will die.' " "You will not surely die," the serpent said to the woman. "For God knows that when you eat of it your eyes will be opened, and you will be like God, knowing good and evil." When the woman saw that the fruit of the tree was good for food and pleasing to the eye, and also desirable for gaining wisdom, she took some and ate it. She also gave some to her husband, who was with her, and he ate it" (Genesis 3:1–6).

Some people, hearing this story, wonder, "What's the big deal? All of this over a piece of fruit?"

But of course it wasn't just about a piece of fruit. First Eve, and then Adam, chose to trust the serpent rather than God. They chose the word of the serpent over the word of God. And that tore at the most important bond in their perfect world.

Tasting that forbidden fruit was really about a basic trust issue. It was about direct disobedience. It was about a ruptured relationship. It was about violated boundaries. Adam and Eve chose to listen to the voice of an enemy, Satan, speaking through a serpent. They elevated their will above the will of God.

God had created earth's first couple for fellowship. He had entered into an intimate relationship with them based on mutual vulnerability and trust. In the beginning God and this first human couple were happily committed. But one sad day they chose to break that commitment and break the relationship of trust. And things would never be the same again.

After tasting what was out of bounds for the first time, Adam and Eve tasted guilt, sorrow, shame, and misery for the first time. "Then the eyes of both of them were opened, and they realized they were naked; so they sewed fig leaves together and made coverings for themselves" (Genesis 3:7).

These two people had enjoyed a relationship of innocent beauty. Now shame and distrust made them want to avoid, to hide, to conceal. It fractured their relationships with each other and with God. Before that fateful day, they had always looked forward to God their Father and Creator coming by for a visit. They loved conversing with Him. But now something made them afraid. "Then the man and his wife heard the sound of the LORD God as he was walking in the garden in the cool of the day, and they hid from the LORD God among the trees of the garden" (Genesis 3:8).

Shame makes people try to do the impossible: hide from God. It short-circuits the chemistry of face-to-face fellowship. Adam and Eve knew they had broken their covenant relationship with God, and they couldn't escape that bitter, nauseating taste of remorse and fear.

"But the LORD God called to the man, 'Where are you?' He answered, 'I heard you in the garden, and I was afraid because I was naked; so I hid' " (Genesis 3:9, 10).

I remember the day Bill and Jane came into my office and sat down for counseling. I could feel the tension between them. Jane had received a call from another woman, who confessed she was having an affair with Bill. Jane felt devastated, of course. Bill had denied everything when she confronted him.

There in my office, Jane tearfully talked about what a terrible blow this adultery was to their marriage. And Bill continued claiming that he'd been faithful.

Well, I had to do what I could to get to the bottom of this very sticky situation. Jane and Bill needed help. Eventually the truth came out. The other woman had made it all up. She'd been nursing secret fantasies about Bill. And she wouldn't let them go. She wanted to destroy this marriage in order to have a chance at Bill someday.

It took some work, but eventually trust was restored. And in this case, Jane had to face a hard truth. Her decision to trust the word of the other woman (without any evidence) rather than the word of her husband almost destroyed her marriage.

That's essentially what happened in the Garden of Eden. Adam and Eve trusted in the wrong voice. There was no evidence that God had ever held anything back from them. There was no evidence this serpent had anything better. But they wandered away from God's guidance—and walked over a cliff. They fell into brokenness. Sin damaged their relationship as a couple. They began blaming each other for the tragedy.

"And [God] said, 'Who told you that you were naked? Have you eaten from the tree that I commanded you not to eat from?' The man said, 'The woman you put here with me—she gave me some fruit from the tree, and I ate it' " (Genesis 3:11, 12).

The subtext behind Adam's response went something like this: "It's all her fault! I sinned, but it's her fault. She gave me the fruit. How was I to know where she got it? And what about You, God? I was just fine in this Garden all by myself, but You had to make this woman and put her here."

24

Eve wasn't about to take the rap either. "Then the LORD God said to the woman, 'What is this you have done?' The woman said, 'The serpent deceived me, and I ate' " (Genesis 3:13).

The message Eve didn't dare say out loud was: "God, You know it's not really my fault. It's that stupid serpent, Lord. He's the one who made me do it! Who put him here, anyway?"

Everybody's passing the buck. Adam and Eve couldn't trust each other. And they couldn't really trust themselves either. They weren't standing together. They were barely standing by themselves.

This first human tragedy points to an issue we all face. We want to be in charge. We want to make the rules. And so God's being in charge and God's making the rules creates a conflict. It's often a hidden conflict, buried inside. But it's there. Too often our relationship with God, or lack thereof, is more a power struggle than a matter of love and trust.

We have a hard time trusting God. We have a hard time giving up control and allowing Him to guide us and teach us and help us grow. We have a hard time when we run up against "Thou shalt not . . ."

A lot of us do seek God, of course. We pray about our challenges and problems. But let's face it, usually this is about our trying to get God to follow our agenda. We've already decided what's best, and we want Him to get on board.

It's just human nature to want to remain the scriptwriter, casting director, choreographer, and producer of the drama of our own lives. And of course we must have the starring role.

But that first human tragedy in Eden is trying to tell us something. It's showing us what happens when God is moved from the center. Everything gets thrown out of whack. Our spirits dry up when we cut ourselves off from the source of life. Human existence is sustained by more than oxygen, water, and food. Each one of us desperately needs God's nourishment. We need that direct link to the Creator. And that means, quite simply, we need to trust. The primary requirement for life is a relationship with God.

How do we maintain that relationship? Jesus once summed it up quite nicely. He said, "If you love Me, keep My commandments" (John 14:15, NKJV). The relationship with God that sustains us begins with love and grows with obedience. It's a healthy process. The more we appreciate about God, the more we want to be like Him.

When that process is interrupted, death results. It doesn't happen immediately, but our souls begin to wither. Several prophets in the Old Testament summed up God's appeals to His people in this way: "Obey and live. Disobey and die." That wasn't an arbitrary divine decree. It was simply the Creator announcing a basic law of life.

Life, real life, depends on an unbroken relationship with God. When that relationship fractures, the natural result is death. That which was intended for eternity becomes temporary.

And that's why what seemed to be a little matter of forbidden fruit in Eden became a tragedy. Adam and Eve were doomed when they bit into it.

But that tragedy placed God in a terrible dilemma. Part of what makes God God is that He is consistent and just and honorable. He doesn't say things and then take them back. He doesn't yell loud warnings and then say, "I didn't really mean it." No, His consistently good character is expressed in the moral laws of the universe. So He couldn't just turn a switch and reverse the process of death caused by disobedience. That is, He couldn't do that and still be Himself.

However, another thing that makes God God is the quality of mercy. He is full of grace as well as full of justice. And that makes it inconceivable that He could simply turn the other way and abandon His children to their fate. He was compelled to do something about that broken relationship—even if human beings were the ones who broke it.

How could the Creator be both just and merciful? In other words, how could He be Himself in the face of sin and death?

Wouldn't you know it, the ingenious Creator came up with a plan. It was something that would allow Him to do the seemingly impossible—act as both lawgiver and rescuer.

God made an announcement. It's found in Genesis 3:15. Speaking to the serpent, He said: "And I will put enmity between you and the woman, and between your offspring and hers; he will crush your head, and you will strike his heel."

This was actually a declaration of war. God declared war on the serpent who had seduced our first human parents. He was going to crush that serpent's head. He was going to do it by sending His Son into the world. He would put "enmity"—hatred—between the serpent and the woman and her offspring, in other words, between the serpent and Eve's descendants, you and I. Eve's "offspring" also refers to a particular descendant, Jesus, who would one day lay His own body down as a barrier between humanity and its mortal enemy.

How? By allowing that evil serpent to strike a blow against Him. The serpent would "strike his heel." Christ would suffer on the cross, paying the price of sin for all of humankind. He would take on the death that justly results from sin. He would absorb in His own flesh its consequences. And He would present His own perfect life as the fulfillment of the law—in our place.

God had come up with a way to restore our relationship with Him—and still express His justice. Human beings would have another chance to trust—by trusting in the One who lived among us, the One who offers complete pardon and acceptance.

And now, this trust can bring us everything we need. Everything from restoration and forgiveness to eternal life.

This is expressed beautifully in the beginning of the Gospel of John. That's where Jesus is called the "Word." Jesus is the Word who became flesh and lived with us and made possible reconciliation between God and man. And John explains just how this happens: "Yet to all who received him, to those who believed in his name, he gave the *right* to become children of God—children born not of natural descent, nor of human decision or a husband's will, but born of God" (John 1:12, 13, emphasis added).

This is the means of reconciliation. By trusting in Jesus' death, we can be reconnected with the Source of life. We can live forever, as children of God.

But notice this verse points out that when we receive Jesus by believing or trusting in Him, God gives us the "right" to become His children. That word *right* is quite remarkable. The Greek word translated as *right* in the New International Version is defined in a typical concordance as "right, power, authority, dominion." Let's look carefully at those four words.

First of all, *right* is a legal term. In the United States, individuals are said to have "certain inalienable rights." If something is ours by right, we have a legal claim to that thing. However, in this world, legal rights are sometimes denied, sometimes crushed. The long, agonizing history of slavery is one example. Those who declared everyone has an inalienable right to freedom denied that right to Africans in America. Some who championed democracy also worked to prevent certain groups from voting because of racial prejudice.

It's one thing to *have* the right, but it's another to actually be able to *exercise* that right. If you aren't able to do so, you might as well not have it.

However, this Greek word *right* also includes the idea of "power." We could translate the verse, "Yet to all who received him, to those who believed in his name, he gave the ***power*** to become children of God."

When you trust in Jesus, not only do you have the *right* to become His child, but you also have the *power* to exercise that right. You have the power to make it happen by virtue of the trust you have placed in Jesus.

So, having the right is good. Being able to exercise the right is better. But best of all is the ability to exercise the right without fear of bad consequences. If we get into trouble because we've exercised a certain right, then it's not much of a right is it?

Well, Jesus took care of that issue as well. There's a third meaning to this Greek word *right*. And that is, "authority." John is telling us that we have the *authority* to become children of God. When you place your trust in Christ, He gives you full *authority* to use the *power* He gave you to exercise your *right* to become His child.

What's more, this wonderful Greek word even contains a promise that we won't ever have to worry about a higher authority revoking this privilege. The fourth idea contained in this word is "dominion." That carries a lot of weight. In other words, you have the *right,* you have the *power* to exercise that right, you have the *authority* to use your power, and that authority is declared to be the ultimate authority—you have *dominion* in this matter.

What a wonderful way to give us assurance as sons and daughters of God! When you place your trust in Jesus Christ, He declares that you are now the ultimate authority in the matter of becoming His child. Your choice seals it. No other person or earthly power can revoke this privilege since Jesus has declared that your trust in Him grants you ultimate dominion in matters of your eternal life.

That's rock-solid assurance. That's something to rely on and trust in. Your salvation is absolutely, rock-solidly sure!

On day six of the ill-fated mission of Apollo 13, the astronauts realized they would have to make a critical course correction. If they didn't get it just right, they might never return to Earth. In order to conserve power, they would have to shut down the onboard computer that steered the craft. And then they would have to initiate a thirty-nine-second burn of the main engines at precisely the right time.

But how to steer?

Astronaut Jim Lovell determined that if they could keep a fixed point in space in view through their tiny window, they might be able to steer the craft manually.

That focal point turned out to be their destination—Earth.

The hit movie *Apollo 13* dramatized those thirty-nine agonizing seconds. It showed us the astronaut pilot intensely focused on keeping the earth in view. And the maneuver worked. All those courageous astronauts made it home. They avoided disaster by not losing sight of that reference point.

There's a very similar way in which we can finish our life mission successfully. The writer of Hebrews tells us about it: "Fix our eyes on Jesus, the author and perfecter of our faith" (Hebrews 12:2).

Keep your eyes on Jesus. There's so much wisdom in that simple admonition. It's how we keep connecting to something rock-solid. It's how we can absorb grace. It's how we can be assured of our acceptance with God. It's how we grow.

Oswald Chambers once wrote: "It is not our trust that keeps us, but the God in whom we trust who keeps us."

Adam and Eve made the wrong choice. And they sent human history spiraling off toward disaster. But we have the opportunity to allow Christ to reverse our particular human story and to head our lives toward wholeness.

In 1983, the United States issued a postage stamp commemorating the building of the first steel bridge in America. It spanned the great Mississippi River at St. Louis. Before work on the project began, many predicted such a structure just couldn't be built—not with all that steel. The bridge would never support its own weight, much less the weight of a train filled with passengers.

So, right after the span was completed, James Eads, the builder, had fourteen locomotives roll out onto the bridge and stop. They just sat there all day long. Well, the people of St. Louis finally realized the bridge could be trusted. They began calling it the eighth wonder of the world.

When Christ laid His body down on the cross of Calvary, He became a bridge between heaven and earth, between sinful humanity and a holy God. And for two thousand years He has proven Himself trustworthy. Countless individuals have placed the weight of their trust on that broken body. And Christ has sustained them all. The wealthy and the impoverished, scholars and peasants, former mobsters and aspiring saints, young children and grandparents—millions around the world have laid down their lives on that bridge, and it has held them all.

The key to life is trusting Christ. Jesus' words to Nicodemus ring out for each one us: "Whoever believes in the Son has eternal life" (John 3:36). That verse could be translated, "Whoever *trusts* in the Son has eternal life." Trusting in Christ brings life. Refusing to trust Christ results in death. The verse continues, "but whoever rejects the Son will not see life, for God's wrath remains on him."

Many people down through the ages have testified that trusting in Christ really does bring life. They've said they began to live when they began a relationship with Him. Countless people, standing on that bridge, have declared that they wouldn't want to stand anywhere else.

When the great reformer John Hus was condemned to the stake, he had to undergo what was called "the ceremony of degradation." Church dignitaries at the scene publicly stripped away his identity as a priest and as a Christian.

First the cup of communion was taken from his hands, accompanied by a formula of deprivation. John Hus, however, cheerily responded by saying, "I hope to drink from the cup in the kingdom of God."

Next the officials removed his garments one by one, pronouncing in each instance the appropriate curse. Hus replied that he was quite willing to suffer shame for the name of the Lord.

Finally a tall paper crown was placed on his head. It pictured three devils fighting for possession of a soul, and read, "This is a heresiarch."

The bishops intoned a final curse: "We commit your soul to the devil!"

John Hus calmly replied, "And I commit it to the most merciful Lord Jesus Christ."

What this courageous believer expressed was this: "You can take everything away from me; you can degrade me publicly, but you can't take away the most precious thing in life: my relationship with the Lord Jesus Christ." As he was led to the place of execution, Hus was heard quoting "In thee, O LORD, do I put my trust; let me never be ashamed" (KJV). It was said that this man stepped toward the stake "as if invited to a banquet."

Those who place their trust in Christ are never disappointed—whatever the circumstances. They know that, standing on that bridge, they can walk into eternal life. They are connected to forever with God.

Where are you placing your trust today? Where are you laying down your life?

The Saddest Day

GENESIS 6–8

Dear Diary,

I knew it was coming. I'd even prepared for it, prepared a plan to deal with the worst possible outcome. But still you can't really be ready for the pain, the jagged edge of rejection. These two wonderful human beings I'd breathed life into walked right off a cliff. I couldn't stop them; it was their choice. They swallowed Lucifer's smooth lines. And I knew what I had to do.

This evening I confronted the couple, and they came clean—well, almost. They took turns blaming each other, the serpent, and Me. But they did admit they'd failed to trust My word and tasted the forbidden fruit. That's when I had to send them out of the Garden, that perfect, beautiful home I'd spent many happy hours preparing for them.

It sickens Me to realize they are now mortal, living under the shadow of death. But what's infinitely more horrible is the possibility of their dying without a reconciliation, the possibility of separation for all eternity! It rips at My heart. How precious the sweet moments of face-to-face fellowship we once knew now seem. The loss is sinking in. And it's almost too much to think about the pain and suffering this couple and all their descendants will experience as a result of this tragic choice.

The saddest day.
Signed,
God

If our Creator kept a journal, it might read something like that. If we were to try to imagine His emotions after Adam and Eve fell into sin, they may have been expressed in that way. It was a time of crisis that everyone would long remember.

But a few generations later, the human story got much, much worse. And the pain our Creator experienced deepened. His next journal entries might have sounded like this:

Dear Diary,

Today I have to face the unthinkable. An era is over! All the hopes of heaven for this earth are smashed. The angels are expressing astonishment that it all went so bad so fast. And there's something inside Me like grief over the fact I made man. Their rejection of everything good has become an epidemic—with no end in sight. They're gone and they're not coming back. The pain is overwhelming! If only there was a shred of hope they might return to their senses and to Me! I've searched far and wide to find some redeeming value among these clans spreading out over the face of the earth. I've worked to fan aflame something of My spirit in human hearts everywhere. But the darkness only deepens. There's just one flicker of light—My man Noah. He wants to honor Me. He loves and trusts Me. Now, as I'm preparing for this horrible task, this stopping of the epidemic, I have only Noah to work with. But whatever happens, I will honor his friendship. I won't let that one flickering flame burn out.

Signed,
God

Think for a moment about God's alternatives when He faced the fact that the objects of His great affection had gone too far, had become caught up in permanent rebellion. What does God do when a relationship is damaged beyond repair? What does God do when the ones He has loved tell Him they don't want any part of Him?

Genesis chapter six tells us. This is a very sad entry indeed in the journal of a lonely God.

"The LORD saw how great man's wickedness on the earth had become, and that every inclination of the thoughts of his heart was only evil all the time. The LORD was grieved that he had made man on the earth, and his heart was filled with pain" (Genesis 6:5, 6).

God had created man for the purpose of fellowship. God wanted human friendships. He wanted genuine, open, loving relationships. His heart is so incredibly deep and wide that He longs for more and more people to experience that with Him.

That's why He made man in His own image. He made us so that His personality and our personalities can bond. God actually made us with *His* natural tendencies toward righteousness, purity, and goodness. He made us with *His* capacity for love.

But in order to be truly like Him we also needed freedom of choice. We had to have the ability to choose God or reject God. Without that freedom, love doesn't exist.

A lonely God took a risk when He created man. All of love involves risk.

When a teenage boy asks a girl on that first date, he risks rejection. When a bride says "I do," she takes a risk. Anyone who opens up his heart to someone else takes a risk.

That's what God did. He imposed a limit on His own power by giving man the power of choice. Man could choose to obey or disobey, and God would have to accept his choice. The Danish theologian Søren Kierkegaard wrote, "God has, so to speak, imprisoned himself in his resolve."

God has limited Himself in order to give love room to grow. C. S. Lewis put it this way: "Perhaps we do not realize the problem, so to call it, of enabling finite free wills to co-exist with Omnipotence. It seems to involve at every moment almost a sort of 'divine abdication.' "

In his own character, God is unlimited. He reigns supreme in the universe. He is dependent on nothing else. What He wills, happens. If the world and everything in it suddenly disappeared, God would still be God.

But, in order to nurture real relationships with real people, God abdicated His absolute power. He stepped back. He took a big risk.

Adam and Eve, as free moral agents, started choosing. They made a bad choice. They lost paradise. God promised to restore it someday if they would choose to be reconciled. But then their children's children began making all kinds of bad choices. Human rebellion reached a critical mass. Before long "every inclination of the thoughts of [man's] heart was only evil all the time."

Today we would define this as a kind of psychopathology. The criminal element had taken over. Generations of parents were raising children even more damaged and twisted than themselves. The madness had to stop.

As God looked on all that He had made, He recorded one of the saddest observations of all time: He was "grieved that he had made man."

What kind of grief was that? Was God grieved for selfish reasons? Did He say to Himself, "If I had known this would hurt Me so badly I never would have done it"?

Or did God feel grieved over all the lost potential, lost promise, lost possibilities? Did He grieve over the anguish and agony of human beings spiraling down in wickedness?

I believe God's grief was about what might have been. He grieved that human beings had fallen so far short of their potential. God could see how destructive human existence had become, and would become, as a result of people cutting off their connection with the Source of life.

The Bible tells us simply that God's "heart was filled with pain." It's quite remarkable to realize that God had to go through a grieving process. He was grieving over a lost relationship. You've probably been there.

A marriage begins to fall apart, for example. Say the husband becomes involved with someone else. He says, when confronted, that he'll give up this adulterous affair. But weeks later he still hasn't broken it off; he still maintains contact with the other woman.

The couple tries to work things out; they try counseling for a little while but continue drifting further and further apart.

And then one very sad day the wife wakes up to realize that he's gone too far. He's really not coming back—ever. The relationship is irreparably broken.

When that happens, you have a couple of options:

You can deny the reality of the situation and hold on to the unrealistic hope that somehow, someday, your spouse will come back.

Or, you can acknowledge the obvious and cut that person loose; you can try to bury the dead relationship and go on with life.

Sad as it is, there comes a time when the second option is the healthier of the two choices. And that's what God decided to do. He decided that man had drifted so far from Him that he was never coming back. It was over. The relationship was dead.

And so it was time for God to remove His life-sustaining hand from the relationship and allow the natural consequences of separation to take place. The one thing God would not do was force obedience. He would not step in and take away human choice.

In counseling with parents, I find that many fall into a trap. They set a rule in the house. So the child naturally tests that boundary, breaks the rule. The parent sets the rule again, but enforces no consequences. The child breaks the rule again. Now the parent sets the rule very loudly, with great threats, but still doesn't invest energy in enforcing consequences.

The pattern continues, with the rule regularly broken and the parent nagging and threatening and screaming.

So I encourage a different approach. I encourage the parents to sit down with their children and write out the rules on a piece of paper. Children can participate in a discussion about the rules, but the parents set them. The rules should be few, and they should be clearly stated.

Also, beside each rule, the parents write a consequence for breaking it. They also write down more serious consequences for repeated violations of the rule.

Once all this is written out, the parents and the child sign the paper. Then when the child breaks a rule, the parents refrain from screaming as punishment. Instead they simply say, "Because we love and respect you, we're going to have to enforce this consequence that we've agreed on." They follow through and leave it at that.

Each violation of the rule has an appropriate consequence that's enforced without anger or argument. It takes time and energy to enforce consequences. Usually it hurts the parent more than the child. But a good parent does it anyway—out of love.

God showed Himself a good parent in Genesis. He had clearly warned people of the results of their rebellion. He had spelled out the rules. Then, when repeated disobedience reached the point of no return, God stepped back and permitted the natural consequences to come: a devastating flood. It was as if the earth itself rose up to protest all the corruption and depravity.

But even in this destruction, God had His eye on one glimmer of hope. His lonely heart would not allow Him to give up completely. God focused on one faithful man. "But Noah found favor in the eyes of the LORD" (Genesis 6:8).

Why? Why did Noah shine in the darkest of times? The next verse tells us, "Noah was a righteous man, blameless among the people of his time, and he walked with God" (Genesis 6:9).

Being righteous and blameless was the result, I believe. Walking with God was the cause. Noah chose to walk with God. He chose to maintain a relationship with Him. That's the reason God looked on him as a blameless man. Noah wasn't perfect. No human being ever has been. But God calls him a righteous man—on the basis of their healthy relationship.

Noah chose a relationship, and that means Noah chose life. That's why he survived the great Flood. God provided a means of escape. One day He told Noah, "I am going to put an end to all people, for the earth is filled with violence because of them. I am surely going to destroy both them and the earth. So make yourself an ark of cypress wood; make rooms in it and coat it with pitch inside and out" (Genesis 6:13, 14).

It seems that God gave Noah the blueprints for a great ship, surely bigger than any that existed at the time. He and his three sons set about putting together this huge floating structure. It took them a hundred and twenty years to complete. (Life spans were considerably longer back then, closer to Creation.)

And here we get another glimpse of God extending grace. Because during this time Noah preached to the inhabitants of the earth, warning them of destruction. And he had plenty of hearers. People came from miles around to see this great boat being built in the middle of the desert.

Noah pleaded with people to repent, to make different choices, to turn back to God, to enter a saving relationship with Him. But sadly, in the end, when the ark was complete, only Noah, his wife, his three sons, and their wives entered the ark. They had plenty of pets for company. Animals somehow arrived from all over the land, walking into the ship, two by two.

At length the door was shut, and they all waited inside. Some spectators began to taunt Noah about his boondoggle. But then the raindrops fell and built into a downpour. And the downpour built into a deluge. Underground springs erupted; lakes and rivers joined forces. Water began to cover the surface of the earth.

Interestingly enough, geologists and other scientists tell us that today you find evidence of underwater life—in the most unexpected places. You can find fossils of sea-going creatures hundreds of miles away from any significant body of water.

The Flood was so vast that it took a hundred and fifty days for the waters to recede. But Noah and his family stayed safe in that ship. I'm sure it was a scary ride, but they would survive. "God remembered Noah and all the wild animals and the livestock that were with him in the ark" (Genesis 8:1).

God didn't forget Noah, the man who'd chosen to go against the crowd and hang on to a precious relationship. As Noah and his family stepped out onto dry land at last, God was still God. He was still both just and merciful. He'd satisfied both sides of His character. There had been consequences, terrible consequences for a terrible time of sin. But there was also a way of escape for all who were willing. God's lonely heart could continue to hope for restored relationships.

God is about second chances. When He brings a flood, He provides an ark. It was that way in the beginning; it will be that way in the end. When this earth and all its evil is finally destroyed by fire, God will provide another place of refuge, a holy city, the New Jerusalem, coming down from heaven, a shelter for all who seek escape. God can't help but hold out hope. His lonely heart demands it.

Noah's first act, after leaving the ark, was to worship the God who saved him.

"Then Noah built an altar to the LORD and, taking some of all the clean animals and clean birds, he sacrificed burnt offerings on it. The LORD smelled the pleasing aroma and said in his heart: 'Never again will I curse the ground because of man, even though every inclination of his heart is evil from childhood. And never again will I destroy all living creatures, as I have done' " (Genesis 8:20).

The aroma that smelled so sweet to God was the aroma of worship. God's heart filled with joy because someone He'd created was responding wholeheartedly. So God made a promise, and He gave that promise a beautiful shape in the sky, the shape of a rainbow:

> Then God said to Noah and to his sons with him: "I now establish my covenant with you and with your descendants after you. . . . Never again will all life be cut off by the waters of a flood; never again will there be a flood to destroy the earth." And God said, "This is the sign of the covenant I am making between me and you. . . . I have set my

rainbow in the clouds, and it will be the sign of the covenant between me and the earth. Whenever I bring clouds over the earth and the rainbow appears in the clouds, I will remember my covenant between me and you and all living creatures of every kind" (Genesis 9:8, 9, 11–15).

Here we see once again God being gracious by limiting Himself. His justice demands that He oppose evil implacably. Yet He promises to disarm Himself. He will take away for all time one certain consequence. He will not destroy all life by means of a flood.

That promise was tested some time later at the Tower of Babel. Then it seemed that humankind was conspiring against the good again. But God chose a different consequence. He split up the conspirators by splitting up their common language into a welter of dialects. When they dispersed, God had prevented evil from reaching a critical mass.

Ultimately, God's solution to the problem of the evil was to absorb it in His own body. On the cross, God's Son took on the consequences of sin and degradation. This would become our ultimate means of escape in a doomed planet. For all who choose to walk with Him, this lonely God provides protection, deliverance, forgiveness, and the hope of perfect, uninterrupted fellowship.

But this doesn't come cheap. It cost God plenty. The Cross impales one eternal principle in the heart of this world: Forgiveness is a costly thing. It's never merely a case of God saying, "It's all right; it doesn't matter." It's never a case of God pretending sin didn't happen. Forgiveness is the most costly commodity in our world. C. S. Lewis wrote: "It costs God nothing, so far as we know, to create nice things; but to convert rebellious wills cost Him crucifixion."

Dear Diary,

Today, I watched My Son die. It wasn't a quick death. I had to stand by as callused hands bruised Him and nailed Him and broke Him. And I couldn't do a thing. If it was truly to be finished, I couldn't intervene. As bad as it was, it got worse. The most wrenching moment: My beloved One and Only crying out to Me, utterly forsaken. And I didn't say a word. I couldn't comfort. I couldn't command the forces of evil to back down. He had to take it all, the whole crushing weight. How I long for My children to be able to look into My heart and understand. How I want them to see the grace that blossoms here in this place of execution and to see the love that blooms where it has been buried under so much cruelty.

Signed,
God

God did the unthinkable. He abandoned His Son. And He did it to offer us a way of escape. He offers it to the most unworthy, to the most indifferent, to the hardest hearts. He offers this infinitely costly thing called forgiveness.

On March 10, 1748, John Newton awakened suddenly to find his cabin rapidly filling with water. A violent sea had crashed into the British trader *Greyhound* and torn away the upper timbers on one side. Above deck the cry went up that the ship was sinking fast.

Newton rushed up and joined other sailors desperately working the pumps, but the sea continued to gain on them, filling the ship. Some began to bail frantically with buckets and pails. Others grabbed clothes and bedding to try to plug numerous leaks.

Newton continued working the pumps through the early morning hours until noon, tying himself to the deck with a rope in order not to be washed away with the passing waves that actually broke over his head. Every time Newton felt the ship settle into a trough, he expected her to sink for good into the deep.

At one point he reported on the crew's desperate efforts to the captain and said, almost without thinking, "If this will not do, the Lord have mercy on us."

Instantly his own words struck him uncannily. What right did he have to ask for mercy? It occurred to him that if the Christian religion had any truth at all, he could not be forgiven.

Newton had been a studious child who liked to sing hymns at his pious mother's knee. But as a teenager he strayed from religious faith about as far as one can. He became a rebellious sailor who fought with anyone who crossed him and indulged in every appetite. As he put it, "I believe for some years I never was an hour in any company without attempting to corrupt them."

Pressed into the British navy, he deserted. Arrested by a military patrol, he was flogged and transferred to a slave trading ship. There he became "exceeding vile."

Newton, now a militant atheist, regularly selected females from among the starving, suffocating slaves wedged in the hold, and raped them. When the ship landed in Sierra Leone, he left it to work for a slave dealer. But soon he became virtually a slave himself on the man's plantation.

Newton's father asked slave-ship captains to keep a lookout for his son on their voyages. In February 1747, the *Greyhound* put in at Sierra Leone, and, through what would later seem providential circumstances, its crew found the young man.

So John Newton, furiously working pumps in the midst of a storm, did not expect rescue. Why should the One he continually and willfully cursed show mercy? An early death seemed an eminently just end to his miserable life.

But somehow the *Greyhound* stayed afloat and limped into Liverpool. "Taking in all circumstances," Newton recalled, "it was astonishing . . . that any of us survived to relate the story." His astonishment turned into a glimmer of faith. He thought of the way he'd been rescued in Sierra Leone; he saw the waves inundating the *Greyhound* in vain, and "I began to know there is a God that hears and answers prayer . . . though I can see no reason why the Lord singled me out for mercy."

Much later, as a beloved minister in England, Newton memorialized God's interventions in the life of a sworn enemy with the words,

> Amazing grace! How sweet the sound!
> That saved a wretch like me.

Sometimes consequences turn on a dimly burning light. Sometimes the flood itself turns us toward our rescue. God is willing to use any means for His gracious purposes. His eyes are roving over the earth, eager to find favor, eager to find a way to awaken the hopeless with mercy. His lonely heart demands that He fashion salvation out of the darkest circumstances so that many, many of His children, like Noah, will be able to walk in the light with Him.

The First Faith Journey

GENESIS 12:1–9

The richest man in the world lay dying. Longtime employees stood ready to heed his every beck and call. His private jet could have taken him anywhere in the world on a moment's notice. His limitless financial resources could have brought in the most skilled medical personnel, the best medical technology.

But Howard Hughes died miserably—a paranoid, skin-and-bones shadow of his former self, completely isolated in a Las Vegas hotel suite.

Brian Piccolo died very differently. This second-string running back for the Chicago Bears wasn't well known and didn't have much financial clout. He couldn't surround himself with the best medical technology. He just had one thing: a faithful friend, fellow running back Gale Sayers, at his bedside.

But that one thing made all the difference. Brian Piccolo died a hero in the eyes of much of America, widely loved and admired because of what he'd come to mean to Gale. Their friendship would be celebrated in the film *Brian's Song*.

Howard Hughes's final days would not be celebrated. Everyone wondered why he had sunk into such bizarre behavior in the end: lying naked on a filthy bed with long beard and matted hair, refusing to be touched, handling objects only with tissue paper. Why?

And the answer was simply that he had no one really close to him, no one who could tell him, friend to friend, "Something's not right here; you need to face reality." During all his life, he never let people get close.

Relationships make all the difference. Do you have people you can open up with, heart to heart? Do you have friendships that are fulfilling?

Ralph Waldo Emerson wrote, "A friend is a person with whom I may think aloud." Do you have friends who allow you to express your thoughts without condemning you or putting you down?

Elbert Green Hubbard wrote, "A friend is one who knows all about you and likes you just the same." Do you have a friend who likes you even when you don't much like yourself?

Aristotle wrote, "What is a friend? A single soul dwelling in two bodies." Real friendship involves a meeting of minds and hearts, a shared identity.

The first patriarch, whose story is told in Genesis, earned an interesting nickname. James 2:23 tells us about it: "And the scripture was fulfilled that says, 'Abraham believed God, and it was credited to him as righteousness,' and he was called God's friend."

Abraham, the father of faith, was called God's friend. That sounds like a wonderfully exclusive title. But the fact is, in Genesis, the journal of a lonely God, we find the Creator had been looking for friends from the beginning.

He wanted to bond with the first human couple. But Adam and Eve broke faith and tried to hide away from Him in the Garden. He tried to reach out to humanity through the preaching of Noah. But thousands turned their backs on Him and marched off to their doom in the Flood.

Finally, however, God spotted someone who seemed to have the capacity for a close relationship. Abram (later to be called Abraham) lived just outside the city limits of Ur, in Chaldea. Ur may sound like some sleepy, one-syllable, backwater town in the wilderness. But in its day, Ur was a cosmopolitan center of culture and commerce. It was likely located at the point where the Euphrates River emptied into the Persian Gulf.

In the thousands of years since Abram's time, the Euphrates has deposited quite a bit of silt. So, today, the point where Ur stood as a port city is about a hundred miles inland.

Back then the city on the sea was surrounded by rich farmland, irrigated by the Tigris and Euphrates Rivers. It boasted a warm climate and lush grasslands for grazing cattle and sheep. Ships sailing out of Ur traded its bounty for goods all along the shores of the Indian Ocean.

The city also served as a center for moon worship. This religious practice involved plenty of idolatry and some rather degraded worship rituals. Not a few of Ur's citizens were headed toward the kind of utterly corrupt lifestyle that had brought on the Flood four centuries before.

Abram's family traced its ancestry back to the sons of Shem. They'd come to Ur after the mass migrations that started at the Tower of Babel; Abram's father Terah would come to lead one of the clans that prospered in the rich farmlands outside the walled city. Some in Terah's family fell into the sexual excesses involved in moon worship. We get a suggestion of that in Genesis 31. That chapter tells us that household idols were found among the possessions of Terah's brother.

Abram was born in this environment. But as he grew up in Ur, it appears that he remained untouched by its corruption. In Hebrew tradition we find stories about Abram's opposition to the idolatrous customs of his time and place. The stories describe Abram making fun of the practice of bowing down to pieces of wood carved as idols or entrusting your life to the moon. His sarcasm provoked the wrath of the king of Ur.

These particular stories are not in the Bible record. But they may help explain why God chose Abram for His special purposes. "The LORD had said to Abram, 'Leave your country, your people and your father's household and go to the land I will show you' " (Genesis 12:1).

Quite a dramatic call. But what kind of call was it? It sounds a bit like asking someone to travel under sealed orders. That happens quite a bit in the military. You are ordered to go to this point and fly to that place and then ship off somewhere else. You open a series of orders, one at a time, that tell you only where to go next.

God was telling Abram to leave the place of his birth, the place where he'd grown up, the place where he'd married and built up his flocks and herds. Everyone and everything Abram knew and loved was in Ur. And what's more, he was supposed to leave and go—somewhere. Surely Abram must have had questions.

"How will I earn a living in the place You're sending me? Does it have good pasture?"

"What's the climate like? You know how I hate cold weather."

"Is it a safe place for all my clan?"

And if Abram's wife, Sarai, was anything like most women, she had questions of her own.

"What kind of home will we live in?"

"What will the people be like there? Will we feel isolated?"

"Will we ever see our friends and family again?"

But there were no answers for Abram or Sarai. God just said, "Go!"

Remarkably, Abram accepted the call. "So Abram left, as the LORD had told him; and Lot went with him. Abram was seventy-five years old when he set out from Haran. He took his wife Sarai, his nephew Lot, all the possessions they had accumulated and the people they had acquired in Haran, and they set out for the land of Canaan, and they arrived there" (Genesis 12:4, 5).

Abram set out—traveling under sealed orders. And this strongly suggests he had a prior relationship with the God of heaven. There had to be an element of trust there. God was confident enough to issue a bold demand. Abram was comfortable enough to go into the unknown.

But he wasn't following a blank. He was following a great promise. This is what God said to him:

> I will make you into a great nation
>   and I will bless you;
> I will make your name great,
>   and you will be a blessing.
> I will bless those who bless you,
>   and whoever curses you I will curse;

and all peoples on earth
    will be blessed through you (Genesis 12:2, 3).

God trusted Abram to become the father of a great nation, a nation whose purpose would be to invite the entire world into a relationship with a lonely God. And Abram, seventy-five years old at the time, started on a great adventure. He had a lot of relatives, but he was childless. Having no son, it must have been hard for this old man to imagine an entire nation of descendants.

Still, Abram stretched out and believed God could do the impossible. That's one reason James would later tell us that Abraham was known as God's friend. Ralph Waldo Emerson wrote, "The only way to have a friend is to be one." What's true of human friendships is true of friendship with God. Abram chose to be God's friend.

When Abram arrived in the land God had promised him, he found that someone else owned it—the Canaanites. God hadn't mentioned that!

But He was still making promises. "The LORD appeared to Abram and said, 'To your offspring I will give this land.' So he built an altar there to the LORD, who had appeared to him" (Genesis 12:7).

At the time, that may have sounded like a pretty empty promise to a homeless, childless, seventy-five-year-old man. But Abram believed again. He built that altar. He worshiped.

Why? That's what friends do. They believe each other even when it's difficult—even when the external evidence points against it! " 'Abraham believed God, and it was credited to him as righteousness,' and he was called God's friend" (James 2:23).

Abram believed God when he had to leave the comfort of family and friends.

Abram believed God when he was journeying into the unknown.

Abram believed God when he arrived alone in a strange land.

Abram believed God when God was making promises out of thin air.

That was the one constant in his life. And he was called God's friend.

It's a great thing to be called God's friend. How do we achieve that distinction? It's closer than you think. It's simply a matter of trust. You believe God's promises. You take Him at His Word.

People today are hungry for genuine friendships. One reason is that we're more and more connected solely by technology. True, we can communicate by email and cell phone with all kinds of people just about anywhere, anytime. But we still long for that deeper face-to-face contact.

More and more, education is about "distance learning." Students at "remote campuses" face a screen on which a professor lectures them from several time zones away. More and more, office workers are confined to communicating through modems and fax machines in cubicles or even at home. Our paychecks are deposited electronically. We pay bills online. We can shop on Web sites and send birthday or anniversary greetings by email cards.

Our high-tech world has become a low-touch society. We long for the personal touch, for the warmth of abiding relationships.

And amazingly enough, that makes us a lot like God. That's part of His image in us. He longs for the same things we long for. But what's different about God is that He can offer so much more than any one human being. He can offer a friendship that's eternal both in quantity and quality.

Thomas à Kempis wrote this about friendship with Christ: "When you have Christ, you are rich. He is enough. He will provide everything you need so you won't have to count on others without him. People change and fail. You cannot depend on them. Those that are for you today may be against you tomorrow. They are as variable as the wind. But Christ is eternally faithful."

So how do we plug into this forever kind of friendship with God? Our most important clue comes from a low-tech nomad on his way to Canaan. Abram stretched on his tiptoes and gave God all the faith he had. He put it out there. And he became God's dear friend.

As simplistic as it may sound, believing God is the essential building block in a meaningful relationship with Him. But this belief isn't just a nod toward heaven. It's a challenge. It's a call to put it out there.

Believe God when you can't see how His promises can possibly be fulfilled.

Believe God when people around you are sure His principles are outdated.

Believe God when your impulses drive you in the opposite direction.

Believe God when you're hurting, frightened, and alone.

Believe God when He calls you to take a radical step in your life.

One day in 1961 a Christian believer in Siberia had a very unusual dream. It seemed that God was calling him to go to Moscow, where he would find a Bible for the church he attended. The man resisted the idea at first. This was a time when the Soviet empire was intent on suppressing Christian faith. The man knew that Moscow's churches had precious few Bibles of their own. But the dream had seemed so vivid and authoritative. And he kept thinking of his 150 fellow church members without a single copy of Scripture among them.

So this Siberian embarked on a journey of faith. He traveled two thousand miles across the tundra—under sealed orders.

About that time another believer, known as Brother Andrew, started a trip from Holland with his companion Hans. They drove their VW down through Poland, crossed the border into Russia at Brest, and traveled on seven hundred miles to Moscow. These men were also on a journey of faith. They felt called by God to take Bibles into the communist heartland.

Soon after arriving in the city, Andrew and Hans decided to check out the midweek service at a certain Baptist church. They hoped to make contacts there so that they could unload some of their hot merchandise. The scores of Bibles tucked away in their car had somehow made it past border checkpoints and prying guards.

Even so, distributing the books was as risky as slipping them through the Iron Curtain. It's not like you could advertise. And you never knew who might be a KGB informant in a church or even if the pastor was under pressure to report everything. So when Andrew and Hans walked into the Thursday night meeting carrying a sample Russian Bible, they had formed a plan.

After the service the two lingered in the vestibule checking out the twelve hundred worshipers milling past. Each man prayed separately that God would direct him to someone they could safely entrust with their smuggled Scriptures.

Soon Andrew spotted a thin, balding man in his forties standing against the wall. He felt a familiar "moment of recognition." The directive to talk to the man seemed very clear, but Andrew waited for Hans to inch over towards him. Before Andrew could speak, his companion said, "I've spotted our man!" In that vestibule crowded with hundreds of people, Hans nodded toward the worshiper Andrew had chosen.

With hearts thumping, they walked up to the stranger and attempted to introduce themselves and explain where they'd come from. He only stared at them, perplexed, until he caught the word "Dutch." It turned out he spoke German. So the three began a vigorous conversation in that language.

Andrew and Hans listened incredulously as the man told his story. This was the believer who'd come all the way from Siberia to find a Bible for his church, believing that God would somehow come through on the dream. Hans had the privilege of delivering the good news: "You were told to come eastward for two thousand miles to get a Bible, and we were told to go westward two thousand miles carrying Bibles to churches in Russia. And here we are tonight, recognizing each other the instant we meet."

When Hans handed the Siberian one of the Russian Bibles, he was speechless. He stared at the Book, then at the two westerners, then back at the Book. Finally it all sank in, and he burst out with a stream of thanks and gave them bear hugs. Andrew managed to calm him and whispered that there were more Bibles; he could have a dozen to take back home the next morning.

God longs to take you on a wonderful adventure. He wants to take you on a journey of faith. It all begins with a step forward in believing. It begins when you stretch out to trust God as a friend.

Hagar, Lost and Found

GENESIS 16

Deborah Tannan writes a wonderful story about her great-aunt. For many years this woman had been a widow. But in her seventies, she fell in love again. True, she didn't fit most people's picture of someone caught up in a great romance. The woman was overweight and losing her hair; her hands and legs had begun to twist with arthritis.

But she'd found, or rather been found by, the man of her dreams. He was a gentleman in his seventies who loved her dearly. Although he was generally confined to a nursing home, he managed to get out on many weekends to visit her.

Deborah often heard her great-aunt talk excitedly about her rendezvous with her "boyfriend." In trying to explain what the relationship meant to her, she related one conversation in particular.

She'd been dining out with friends one night. After returning home, her friend called on the phone, and she told him all about her pleasant evening. He listened with great interest and then asked, "What did you wear?"

At this point in telling the story, Deborah's great-aunt began to cry. After composing herself she said, "Do you know how many years it's been since anyone asked me what I wore?"

For the first time in decades, this woman felt cherished. Someone was interested in everything about her; someone wanted to listen to her stories; someone wanted all the details. And it was wonderful.

Every human being, no matter their age, no matter their appearance or background, longs to feel cherished. And most of us know the pangs of feeling unloved at times, the pain of being truly alone.

It happens when a relationship breaks up. It happens at a gravesite. It happens when a doctor says "cancer." It happens when your friends are saying "I do," and you still haven't found the right one. It happens when you lose a job or get in financial trouble.

If things get really bad, you start believing that no one *could* love you. You're simply undesirable, not someone to be pursued.

But as it turns out, the journal of a lonely God has good news for those in this situation. There's good news for the rejected in Genesis. It begins with the story of a girl named Hagar.

"Now Sarai, Abram's wife, had borne him no children. But she had an Egyptian maidservant named Hagar; so she said to Abram, 'The LORD has kept me from having children. Go, sleep with my maidservant; perhaps I can build a family through her.' Abram agreed to what Sarai said. So after Abram had been living in Canaan ten years, Sarai his wife took her Egyptian maidservant Hagar and gave her to her husband to be his wife. He slept with Hagar, and she conceived" (Genesis 16:1–4).

At first this story sounds pretty bizarre. I don't know of any woman today who, having failed to conceive, would tell her husband, "Well, honey, how about trying to have a baby with someone else?"

Obviously customs were quite different back then. In fact, the pressure to produce a male heir for her husband was enormous. Also, wealthy men of the time often had more than one wife. It was a practice with very unfortunate consequences, as we shall see.

Sarai was trying to fulfill what she thought was an obligation. The humiliation of not having a son seemed greater than the pain of her husband's taking another wife.

Abram went along with this and took Hagar as his wife. We don't hear too much about Hagar's feelings. She was just a servant girl, a healthy young servant girl quite able to bear children.

Over the years, I've spoken with many young women about their hopes and dreams for marriage. I've asked them do describe their ideal mate, their Prince Charming. I've yet to hear anyone describe someone like Abram—a man in his eighties, someone with a belly, a receding hairline, and a lot of wrinkles.

But Hagar got Abram. At least he was well off. And in that day, other young women might even have envied her new standing as the wife of the head of a prosperous clan.

Hagar did become pregnant, as expected, and this brought her much joy. Finally something good and natural had happened.

Not much had gone right for Hagar through her life. She was born a slave in Egypt. That meant she would always be poor, always at the mercy of other people's whims. She'd never been able to make her own decisions.

And Hagar was not the kind of person who just accepted her lot. She hated being a slave and had tried to run away from her masters more than once. We know that because her name means "fleeing," or "runaway."

Hagar had come into the employ of Abram while he was in Egypt. He may have purchased her; she may have been a diplomatic gift from someone. But she'd become Sarai's handmaiden. And one day, quite unexpectedly, she found herself Abram's wife.

What's more, she was Abram's pregnant wife and feeling pretty good about it. Hagar began to despise Sarai, her barren mistress. The Hebrew word translated "despise" in Genesis 16:4 has an equivalent in today's slang—trash talk. Hagar, the long-oppressed slave, could finally make snide remarks about her aging mistress. She made noises about replacing her as queen bee of the household.

Well, Sarai wasn't about to stand for that. So she took her complaint against Hagar to her husband. "Then Sarai said to Abram, 'You are responsible for the wrong I am suffering. I put my servant in your arms, and now that she knows she is pregnant, she despises me. May the LORD judge between you and me' " (Genesis 16:5).

Sarai kept complaining. She wept; she whined. Finally the old patriarch gave in.

" 'Your servant is in your hands,' Abram said. 'Do with her whatever you think best' " (Genesis 16:6).

Abram was saying that he wouldn't take up the cause of the woman who was bearing his child. He wouldn't stand between her and his wife. Before Hagar had been Sarai's slave. Then she became her rival. Now she would be back under her control. Sarai didn't waste any time paying Hagar back for her disdain. "Then Sarai mistreated Hagar; so she fled from her" (Genesis 16:6).

Whatever Sarai did must have been pretty bad. It drove Hagar back to her old desperate measures. She ran away. She'd reached that point of believing no one cares, of feeling she was utterly alone.

People have always tried to run away from pain. It may be a geographical move: You think your life will be so much better if you can just move to a better neighborhood, a better town. It may be a melodramatic move: You lose it; you explode—and if you get angry enough and loud enough, then people may back off and not force you to deal with your real problems. It may even be a productive move: You submerge yourself in work so you don't have to talk about those unresolved conflicts with your loved ones. Or it may be a self-destructive move: You numb yourself with alcohol or drugs until the pain seems like a hazy thing in the distance.

The good news is, there are lots of ways to run. The bad news is, your problems always catch up with you. Psychologists tell us that about 90 percent of our problems have nothing to do with our circumstances—the external pressures in our lives. We all would love to have something or someone else to blame, of course. But the truth is *we* have to own the problem. We have to own the anger or the disconnection or the manipulative behavior. As the comic strip character Pogo said, "We have met the enemy, and he is us!"

Hagar found herself wandering out in the desert one hot afternoon. And she had good reason to be wandering. There was much in this woman's story that makes us want to cheer on her escape. And yet even this abused individual needed to do something more than just run. She needed to confront her real problem.

God decided to help her do that. The lonely God loved this lonely woman and followed her out of camp and into the desert. He pursued her because God knows what it is to be a friend. He sent an angel to perform an intervention. "The angel of the LORD found Hagar near a spring in the desert; it was the spring that is beside the road to Shur. And he said, 'Hagar, servant of Sarai, where have you come from, and where are you going?' " (Genesis 16:7, 8).

The road to Shur was actually the way back to Egypt. Hagar was trying to get home, though it's doubtful she ever had much of a home or much of a family. She was trying to get back to something familiar.

But God had better plans. First of all, the angel called her by name, "Hagar, servant of Sarai." She wasn't a nobody out there in the desert. Somebody knew her name. And this somebody, this angel, asked her to open up. "Where have you come from, and where are you going?"

Those are not bad questions to ask when we find ourselves running away. "Where have you come from, and where are you going?" Christian author Ellen White once wrote that the only thing we have to fear is that we forget God's leading in our past.

Where have you come from? Is there any evidence that God has blessed you in the past or led you in the past? Has He been there? Has He cared for you, perhaps even when you were unaware?

Don't forget who you are. Never forget where you've come from.

And what about where you're going now? Where is this road going to take you? As the saying goes: "Unless you change course, you can expect to end up exactly where you are headed today."

This is what the angel asked Hagar. And, interestingly enough, Hagar was honest with the angel. She didn't try to hide her sad story. " 'I'm running away from my mistress Sarai' " (Genesis 16:8).

Hagar was running away. But, really, where was she running from? There was more to Abram's household than a jealous mistress. This was a place where the God of heaven was worshiped. This was an island of covenant love in a sea of idolatry. Hagar had learned about God at Abram's feet. True, she was running away from conflict. But she was also running away from the blessings of the chosen.

And where was she going? Back to Egypt. But what had Egypt ever done for her? It represented the old way of life, a more corrupt way of life. Hagar was running away from God back to the familiar, but it was the familiar dysfunction of sin. Hagar probably had not thought of it quite that way. But this is what the angel wanted her to see. He wanted her to see where her present course of action was taking her. Running might relieve some of the pressure of the moment. But it would ultimately lead her away from God.

A lonely God wasn't going to just stand by and watch that happen. He wasn't about ready to give up on her. He wanted her to know what it's like to be cherished. That's why he was pursuing her out there in the middle of nowhere.

The angel proposed a one-step program of rehabilitation. "Then the angel of the LORD told her, 'Go back to your mistress and submit to her' " (Genesis 16:9).

Those must have been hard words to hear. "Go back? Submit?" she might have responded. "Weren't you paying attention? I left because I couldn't take it!"

Hagar had a point. Sometimes we *do* need to leave an unhealthy situation. No one should put up with an abusive relationship. But at other times we need to resolve conflicts; we need to work through power struggles. And this was one of those times.

The angel was insistent. "You can't run away from your problems. You must face them head on."

At that moment, worn out, thirsty, and alone, Hagar didn't have the strength to face those problems. She'd come to the end of her own resources. But this was actually a moment of opportunity. This was her chance to truly face a new day in the strength of her new Best Friend, the God of heaven.

So the angel gave her a promise straight from the Lord. "The angel added, 'I will so increase your descendants that they will be too numerous to count' " (Genesis 16:10).

God was saying that He was welcoming Hagar into covenant blessing. This was like the promise given to Abram. "I will make you into a great nation" (Genesis 12:2). Hagar could have a part in God's special plans. She wasn't just fighting a lonely battle as a powerless slave anymore. God was on her side. She would have success. Her descendants would become too numerous to count.

The down payment of those descendants was now in her womb.

> The angel of the LORD also said to her:
> "You are now with child
>   and you will have a son.
> You shall name him Ishmael,
>   for the LORD has heard of your misery" (Genesis 16:11, 12).

God was letting this woman know, in the days before ultrasound, that she was carrying a boy. She had a male heir, and she was to call him Ishmael. That name means "God hears." Life was coming full circle. "Runaway" would bear a child identified as "God hears." In other words, God is paying attention; God cares. This child is an answer to prayer.

Many nights this girl had cried herself to sleep thinking no one knew what she was going through, thinking her tears would always fall unnoticed in the dark. But now, Someone heard. Someone saw. Someone called her by name. Someone showered her with covenant promises. Her Ishmael would always remind her of that. The promise would be repeated every time she called her son: "God hears, it's time to get up!" "God hears, come in for lunch." "Good night, God hears."

A lonely God does hear the cries of lonely men and women. Those cries register. And God responds. You have never shed a tear that God didn't feel. Your most hidden scars and deepest longings find an echo in the heart of a God who bore all our sorrows on the lonely hill of Calvary. And there is no prayer too faint, no groaning too inarticulate, for Him to decipher. He is truly the God who hears.

God's promise stopped Hagar in her tracks that day. It sunk in. "She gave this name to the LORD who spoke to her: 'You are the God who sees me,' for she said, 'I have now seen the One who sees me' " (Genesis 16:13).

In those words I hear an echo of Deborah Tannan's story about her great-aunt. It's the sentiment of someone who said, "Do you know how many years it's been since anyone asked me what I wore?" Hagar knew that God saw through her, in the very best way. He saw all her pain and loneliness and struggles. He wasn't just the God of Abram anymore, the God of her master. He was her God, on her side. So she called Him a name that had meaning for her—"The God Who Sees Me."

Hagar wanted to make sure she'd always remember this moment of truth. She wanted all those descendants God promised her to remember it. So she also gave the spring of water there her own name. "That is why the well was called Beer Lahai Roi; it is still there, between Kadesh and Bered" (Genesis 16:14).

Beer Lahai Roi means "well of the Living One who sees me." That would always be the place of Hagar's story. And it's a story for all who come to that place in their own experience where no one seems to care, no one seems to notice.

Beth was a young woman who'd been born way out on the wrong side of the tracks. Her mother was a prostitute. Everyone assumed Beth would follow in her mother's footsteps. Maybe she already had.

But something unexpectedly good happened to Beth. She met a young man, fell in love, and married him. He was a young pastor named Jim. He knew all about Beth's embarrassing background. But he cherished her and appreciated the fact that she'd turned her back on the old lifestyle.

Beth didn't want to ever go back. She loved Jim, loved every hour they were together. This man treated her differently than she'd ever been treated before. In his eyes, she was always somebody. He had a tender way of expressing how much she meant to him.

But when the first child came along, something began to change. Maybe it was all those dirty diapers. Maybe it was how tired she felt or the fact that they never seemed to have enough money. Whatever it was, it began to drive a wedge between Beth and Jim. She became more distant. She wasn't quite as spontaneous in her affection.

Jim didn't understand why. He just kept loving his wife and hoping things would get back to the way they were.

Instead, the distance widened. Beth gave birth to a second child, but their life as parents didn't seem to bond them. Beth withdrew more and more into herself.

When she did talk, a stream of resentful words came out. She resented being so poor; she resented the constant attention her toddlers required. And she even seemed to resent Jim's unfailing kindness toward her.

By the time the third baby came along, Jim found himself wondering, during dark, lonely nights, if the child was his. Still, he tried to express his love for Beth every day.

One day Jim came home to find Beth gone and the children alone in the house. Suddenly he knew she wasn't coming back.

His friends said, "Let her go. You have biblical grounds to divorce her and remarry. You need to get on with your life."

But Jim couldn't drown out the longing that still burned in his heart. He set out to find his wife. He visited her family and called on her old friends. No one knew where she might have gone.

Weeks turned into months. Jim couldn't give up his search. And finally, one day he found someone who'd heard of her. But this man didn't have good news. "Jim, it's real bad. She's strung out and sick. Beth has taken up a life that's about as far from that of a pastor's wife as you can imagine."

Still, Jim tracked down a current address and went to see Beth. He found her pale and emaciated, staring out a window with dark, hollow eyes.

Jim touched her arm and whispered, "Beth, it's me. I love you. Please come home."

Beth looked up at him and began weeping uncontrollably. Then, after a long silence, she lifted a skinny arm and pointed to a man sitting in the next room.

He was her pimp. "I owe him money," she said weakly. "Until I pay it, I can't go anywhere."

Jim took a deep breath and asked the man how much Beth owed. He drove to the bank, took out all his savings and just about wiped out the checking account.

Handing the money over to Beth's pimp, he said, "Beth's debt is paid in full. She's my wife. Never touch her again."

Then he picked up the woman he cherished, carried her to his car, and took her home.

It took some time for Beth to heal, physically and emotionally. But Jim poured out his love from that same boundless spring inside him. Whenever she broke down and sobbed about the terrible things she'd done, Jim reminded her that God had forgiven her—and so had he.

Whenever Beth felt so dirty she just couldn't stand it, Jim would hold her in his arms until the feeling went away.

When she talked about how worthless she'd become, Jim told her, "You are my princess. I live for you. You have infinite value in my eyes."

Why was Jim able to rescue his wife? Why was he able to pay such a high price for society's castoff? Because his lonely heart demanded it. His love wouldn't have it any other way.

Jim believed he was polishing a diamond in the rough. Jim believed in Beth's capacity for intimacy.

Jim's story mirrors the story of a lonely God. It's a faint reflection of the great passion that has taken hold of God's heart. He has gone to enormous lengths to bring you back home.

You may feel so undesirable that no one would possibly want to pursue you. God is pursuing you with a passion. You may have turned your back and wandered far from everything good, everything connected to God. But He will stop at nothing to get you back.

His lonely heart insists on it. His love demands it.

Abraham Tested

GENESIS 22

A few years ago, my wife, Gayle, asked what I thought of her organizing a garage sale. I said it was a great idea, if she could find the time. And besides, we could use the money.

There was one little catch to Gayle's request. She wanted to use all the proceeds for whatever she wanted. That was a little curious because Gayle had never asked for anything like that. She's so very unselfish, always thinking of the family first.

It caught me off guard, but I said, "Since you're doing most of the work, it's only fair."

So one weekend Gayle had her garage sale and made over three hundred dollars. I admit that I was a little curious about what she intended to do with the money, but I didn't pry.

A month later Gayle gave me a very special birthday present—two tickets to a performance of *Phantom of the Opera* at Fort Worth's Bass Performance Hall. Gayle knows I love the theater, especially musicals. It was a perfect gift—but I knew it was much more than we could afford. How much more? Three hundred dollars more—precisely what she'd been able to raise through her garage sale.

That's probably the most thoughtful gift I've ever received. It certainly made me feel loved. What's the greatest gift of love you have ever received? What's the greatest gift of love you have ever given?

When Warren Sapp was playing defensive end for the Tampa Bay Buccaneers, he claimed that he loved head coach Tony Dungy. In explaining the depth of his commitment he said, "I would take a bullet for him." And then he added, "If it wouldn't kill me."

Like most of us, Sapp loved—up to a point. His love had limits.

In the journal of a lonely God, however, we find a love without limits. We find a love that's extreme. God Almighty was willing to sacrifice Himself rather than give up on weak, sinful human beings. He made that commitment in His promise about crushing the serpent's head, back in the Garden of Eden. But few people had the capacity to really understand the immensity of God's commitment. They couldn't grasp the breadth and depth of His love. Not even Abraham. Not even the one God had chosen to found a great nation of faith.

So this lonely God decided to give to Abraham, His servant, an object lesson. It was a dramatic picture that future generations would study and admire.

The story is told in Genesis 22. "Some time later God tested Abraham. He said to him, 'Abraham!' 'Here I am,' he replied. Then God said, 'Take your son, your only son, Isaac, whom you love, and go to the region of Moriah. Sacrifice him there as a burnt offering on one of the mountains I will tell you about' " (Genesis 22:1, 2).

Of all the times to tell yourself you're just hearing voices and not hearing God, surely this was one of them. Isaac was the son of promise, the miracle baby Abraham and Sarah had conceived in old age. He was the one through whom God was going to fulfill His promise. He was the heir through whom a great nation would come.

Abraham was over a hundred years old by now, and Sarah was not far behind. It was long past time for him to think about starting over.

The command that this patriarch heard seemed to go against everything he knew about God. Abraham spent a sleepless night tossing and turning. He loved his son with all his heart, and he also loved God with all his soul. What was he to do? I'm sure that he walked out of his tent and looked up at the stars, pleading for clarification or an alternative or a reprieve. But God didn't offer anything.

The morning came far, far too quickly. But when the night was over, Abraham had decided to obey his Lord. He took another very difficult step in his long journey of faith. "Early the next morning Abraham got up and saddled his donkey. He took with him two of his servants and his son Isaac. When he had cut enough wood for the burnt offering, he set out for the place God had told him about" (Genesis 22:3).

The father and son walked through the dry landscape in silence. Isaac, not knowing what was up, enjoyed the exercise. Abraham agonized over every step.

"On the third day Abraham looked up and saw the place in the distance. He said to his servants, 'Stay here with the donkey while I and the boy go over there. We will worship and then we will come back to you.' Abraham took the wood for the burnt offering and placed it on his son Isaac, and he himself carried the fire and the knife. As the two of them went on together, Isaac spoke up and said to his father Abraham, 'Father?' 'Yes my son?' Abraham replied. 'The fire and wood are here,' Isaac said, 'but where is the lamb for the burnt offering?' Abraham answered, 'God himself will provide the lamb for the burnt offering, my son.' And the two of them went on together" (Genesis 22:4–8).

Isaac, who was about sixteen at the time, knew about burnt offerings. He'd helped his father in these acts of worship, offering up a lamb to the God of heaven. So he noticed what was missing. And a lot of sixteen-year-olds wouldn't have been content with Abraham's answer. *God will provide?* Isaac must have thought. *How, out here in this desolate place?* Most kids would have kept on pestering Dad until they got a better explanation.

But Isaac had learned to trust his father. And he'd seen the ways in which God had indeed provided as the family settled in a new land. So he didn't press the issue.

Abraham couldn't bring himself to tell Isaac the whole story. How could any father tell his son such a thing? He just kept hoping against hope that somehow this journey would end happily.

"When they reached the place God had told him about, Abraham built an altar there and arranged the wood on it. He bound his son Isaac and laid him on the altar, on top of the wood" (Genesis 22:9).

"Laid him on the altar"? How did that happen? In between Isaac asking a question and Isaac bound on the altar there must have been a revelation. Abraham must have told Isaac the truth. There was no way this hundred-year-old man could have forced his robust young son up on that altar. Nor would Abraham have wanted to.

Isaac had to do it willingly. We can only guess at Abraham's agonized explanation of the divine command. But Isaac agreed to trust as well. He climbed up on that altar and allowed his father to bind his limbs, like those of a bleating lamb.

There on the top of Mount Moriah, two human beings, trembling, with a knife between them, decided to give God the greatest gift they could offer. "Then he reached out his hand and took the knife to slay his son. But the angel of the LORD called out to him from heaven, 'Abraham! Abraham!' 'Here I am,' he replied. 'Do not lay a hand on the boy,' he said. 'Do not do anything to him. Now I know that you fear God, because you have not withheld from me your son, your only son' " (Genesis 22:10–12).

In a moment, the greatest of gifts turned into the most emotional of embraces. Father and son held each other for a long time on that mountaintop.

But what kind of experience had this really been for them? That question has often been asked. Wasn't Isaac traumatized by the whole ordeal? Why was Abraham asked to make this horrific sacrifice? Just so God could prove his loyalty?

I believe the answer lies in the unique position Abraham occupied in history. Remember he was called to be the father of a nation, and it was to be a nation based on faith. It was to be a nation that could spread God's light through the whole world. And at the center of that light was a sacrifice God Himself was going to make. God Himself was going to give up His only Son. All of Israel's sacrifices pointed to that event. All of Israel's tabernacle services illustrated that great act of love.

And this patriarch was the lone teacher in that moment. He had to make that truth vivid and real for his people, so it could be passed on from one generation to another as a living faith and not become mere tradition.

So how could he communicate the sacrificial love of God powerfully? By getting an unforgettable taste of it himself. After Mount Moriah, Abraham could speak from the heart. He could now speak with passion. He could make God's love vivid, showing it to be the kind of covenant love that holds nothing back.

And Isaac could speak to his children and his children's children in the same way. Yes, it was a scary experience. But there was a meaning to it. It opened up a window into the heart of a lonely God, a God who was willing to sacrifice that which is precious.

Christian writer Ellen White makes this comment on the Genesis account:

> Abraham had greatly desired to see the promised Saviour. He offered up the most earnest prayer that before his death he might behold the Messiah. And he saw Christ. A supernatural light was given him, and he acknowledged Christ's divine character. He saw His day, and was glad. He was given a view of the divine sacrifice for sin. Of this sacrifice he had an illustration in his own experience. . . . Upon the altar of sacrifice he laid the son of promise, the son in whom his hopes were centered. . . . This terrible ordeal was imposed upon Abraham that he might see the day of Christ, and realize the great love of God for the world, so great that to raise it from its degradation, He gave His only-begotten Son to a most shameful death (*The Desire of Ages,* pp. 468, 469).

If we see what happened on Mount Moriah only as a test, it was a cruel test indeed. But it served a much grander purpose. It was an extraordinary experience for a man who had an extraordinary mission.

Abraham played the part of God in a drama that would echo down through history. He embodied a heavenly Father who was willing to give up His Son for a world that didn't seem to care. And Isaac played the part of Christ, obedient to the point of death, death on a cross. And that drama sunk in deep. The father and son would never forget it. And neither would their descendants, the people of Israel, who did indeed become a great nation of faith.

This story isn't about how we live our lives every day. People who hear voices telling them to kill someone are almost certainly not hearing the voice of God. God isn't in the business of asking people to make sacrifices just for the sake of sacrifices. God is in the business of protecting children and families. God is the Life-Giver, not the life-taker.

But in this one extraordinary situation, God did stretch the faith of two human beings so that they could begin to share an extraordinary message of grace to the whole world.

If you've ever wondered about God's love for you, put yourself in Abraham's sandals for a minute and try to imagine what he felt. When you get a small glimpse of that father's anguished torment, then you begin to fathom the wonders of God's love for you.

What is the greatest gift of love you have ever received? It was the gift of Jesus, God's only Son, on Calvary's tree. What is the greatest gift of love you could ever give?

It is the gift of your heart—the gift of yourself—given to God.

Rudyard Kipling liked to take his children for picnics in the hills of Sussex Downs. He played games for hours with them, and he told them stories.

This great British author had fascinated countless readers with tales of life in faraway India, where he had grown up. He became world-famous with the publication of *The Jungle Book* and *Just So Stories.* But nothing gave him greater satisfaction than telling his children stories—like the story of how the leopard got his spots and the zebra his stripes. They wanted to hear that one over and over again.

Kipling adored his two daughters, Josephine and Elsie. And when his wife Carrie bore him a third child, he was overjoyed when the doctor called out, "You have a son."

Now the family was complete. Kipling was determined to give his children a happy childhood, one very unlike his own.

Rudyard was separated from his parents at the tender age of six. He and his sister said farewell in Bombay and were shipped off to England, where they could attend "proper schools." The woman paid to board them had a mean streak. She would beat and taunt Rudyard, who was small and frail for his age. Sometimes he was locked in a cold, damp cellar for hours.

Years later, Kipling determined that his kids were going to have plenty of sunshine. And he enjoyed watching them grow up, playing on the grassy hills of Sussex.

Kipling took special pride in his son, John. He'd always been a bright, cheerful, uncomplaining child. And he developed into a tall, handsome boy, who loved to play rugby.

Kipling loved watching him dash across the field. He was a very proud father—not just because John was a great athlete, but because he showed a quiet courage and good humor. The boy never bragged about a win or whined about a loss.

Kipling realized that his boy was becoming a man. John was living out the values his father had taught him, values that Kipling had seen embodied in many British servicemen stationed in India. He'd always admired their courage, sacrifice, and discipline. Kipling became a rather old-fashioned father, even in the early 1900s, emphasizing honor and dedication to duty. So it gave him joy to see John taking responsibility for his actions. If he broke a rule at school, he took his punishment without complaint, even when it was harsh.

One winter day in 1910 Kipling began to pen some thoughts for his twelve-year-old son. He wanted to express certain ideals to live by. The result was a poem called "If," which would inspire millions. It ended with these words:

> If you can talk with crowds and keep your virtue,
> Or walk with Kings—nor lose the common touch,
> If neither foes nor loving friends can hurt you,
> If all men count with you, but none too much;
> If you can fill the unforgiving minute
> With sixty seconds worth of distance run,
> Yours is the Earth and everything that's in it,
> And—what is more—you'll be a Man, my son!

John Kipling did grow up to be a man. And in 1915, with a war raging in Europe, he decided to do his part. His father managed to get him a commission as a second lieutenant with the Irish Guards.

But then came news of the heavy casualties in the trenches. Wave after wave of recruits were sailing across the channel to France. John might be called to go over any time now. He was eager to serve, but he was only seventeen. He required parental consent to go to the front.

Rudyard Kipling faced an agonizing choice.

He'd visited the front and written about the fighting. He didn't want his son to have to go into that carnage. And yet everything he'd taught the boy about duty and responsibility was moving John in that direction. Rudyard Kipling had been warning about German aggression for years. Now his son wanted to back up his father's words with action.

Finally Kipling gave his consent. On August 15, John waved goodbye from the railing of a ship, with a tip of his officer's cap. His mother thought he looked "very smart and straight and brave."

It was the last time his family would ever see him.

Six weeks later a telegram from the War Office reported, "John Kipling, Missing in Action. Last seen during a battle in Loos, France."

Rudyard Kipling was heartbroken. He tried desperately to learn something, anything, about his son's fate. Traveling to France, he trudged from one muddy outpost hospital to another. He searched among the wounded. He hunted down men from John's battalion.

But he never found his son. He'd been lost in the Great War.

Later Rudyard Kipling would try to deal with his grief by working with the Imperial War Graves Commission. He proposed that a "Stone of Sacrifice" be erected at each cemetery honoring the war dead. It would represent soldiers whose bodies were never identified. It would be inscribed with these words: Known But Unto God.

"Known But Unto God." That memorial was a father's anguished hope that God did know about that lost son, that God did understand.

And God does know all about lost sons. He watched a beloved Son grow into maturity. He too endured a tragedy. He too has a story to tell and a memorial to erect. It's a memorial for each one of us.

When Jesus of Nazareth began to increase in wisdom and stature and in favor with everyone, as Luke tells us, Joseph was proud of his fine Son. But he wasn't the only one. There was another Father, hidden in the shadows, watching over this Boy. There was a heavenly Father who treasured every step His divine Son took toward becoming a man.

But one day, three years later, the heavenly Father had to face a terrible choice. Jesus was agonizing in the Garden of Gethsemane. He was facing a terrible ordeal ahead. He had to make a great sacrifice in the war between good and evil. He had to take on the sins of the world in His own body. It was the only way to make people free.

God didn't want to see His boy suffer. He didn't want to see Him beaten and mocked and spit on. He didn't want to see Him tortured at Golgotha. He would have done anything to spare this beloved Son from that agony.

And yet, everything that this Father and Son believed, everything They stood for, everything They cherished, was moving Them toward the Cross. They had made a pact with each other long before; They had resolved to do whatever it took to rescue human beings from sin and death. And it was going to take this. It was going to take the Cross.

The heavenly Father had to watch His Son be consumed by sin, torn apart by transgression. He had to turn away when His Boy cried out, "My God, My God, why have You forsaken Me?"

A father doesn't forget a cry like that. Those words are seared into his memory.

During the dark days of World War I, Rudyard Kipling had a hard time coming to terms with his loss. He began to wonder if the death of his son had any meaning. Had it made any difference? The fighting dragged on and on.

One day he received a rumpled, brown-paper package in the mail. It was addressed simply to "Monsieur Kipling." The painstaking scrawl indicated it had been sent from the front.

Kipling opened the package and found a red box inside. It contained a French translation of his novel *Kim*. The book had been pierced by a bullet hole—that stopped at the last twenty pages. A string had been tied through the hole, and dangling from it was the Maltese cross, France's medal for bravery in war.

It belonged to a young French soldier named Maurice. He explained in a letter that Kipling's book had saved his life. Had it not been in his pocket when he went into battle, the bullet would have pierced his heart. Maurice asked Kipling to accept the book and the medal as tokens of his gratitude.

Rudyard Kipling had received many honors as a celebrated British author. He'd even won a Nobel Prize for literature. But no honor moved him as much as this one. God had made him a part of sparing someone's life. Maybe there was a meaning to it all. Maybe there was a point to all the sacrifice.

And that is the point to the sacrifice Jesus made. That is the meaning that the heavenly Father sees. Someone's life can be spared. Your life can be spared.

Many lives can be spared.

Rudyard Kipling and that French soldier Maurice kept up a correspondence over the years. They developed a friendship that helped Kipling deal with the loss of his own son. One day Maurice wrote that his wife had given birth to a boy. Would Kipling consent to be the godfather?

Kipling looked out his study window. He remembered that joyful moment when he first held his son in his arms. Now Maurice knew that magical feeling—because his life had been spared. And Kipling realized that no memorial would do more justice to his brave son's memory than this tiny infant, full of promise.

So he wrote back, saying he would be delighted. Rudyard Kipling became the child's godfather. Maurice named him Jean, French for John. And Kipling presented the infant with a gift, that book with the bullet hole in it and the Maltese cross, Maurice's medal. He thought it only fitting that this child should have it.

Do you know what gives God the Father His greatest joy? Do you know what He finds most rewarding about the sacrifice He and His Son made? It's seeing many other children born in faith, born again into the kingdom of heaven. That's the honor that God gives us. He wants us to know that the sacrifice was worth it—because of what it can mean to us.

His was the greatest gift of love the universe has ever seen. And it can inspire us to respond in kind. Love demands that we give ourselves fully, holding nothing back. We may have to sacrifice something. There may be a price for our obedience. But nothing can equal the reward of giving our hearts and souls and minds to the One who gave Himself up for us all.

Fighting for the Birthright

GENESIS 27–28

"The bravery of God in trusting us!" wrote Oswald Chambers. "It is a tremendously risky thing to do."

Have you ever thought that God's trust is a risky venture? The Almighty has, in fact, entrusted us with some very precious things—the gift of His Son, the establishment of His church, the sharing of His gospel around the world.

But the primary way in which God has become vulnerable is simply by offering Himself in relationship with you. He has made the huge investment that makes a relationship possible. He has risked rejection. And He's done it over and over again.

Mother Teresa once said, "I knew God would not give me anything I can't handle. I just wish that He didn't trust me so much."

God trusts so much because the foundation of any close relationship is trust. Before a husband and wife can live together and give themselves freely to each other, they must first trust. Trust implies vulnerability. When we trust someone, we take a risk.

We risk rejection. We risk betrayal. But there's no other way to build an intimate relationship.

And so a lonely God continues to take risks and to make Himself vulnerable.

He does this wanting someone to come along who responds and who proves herself worthy of that divine trust. That person is in for a wonderful surprise. She finds herself in a deeper relationship than she ever thought possible. She finds that God's reward is all out of proportion to her small investment of faith.

If we are to ever fill the loneliness of our hearts, we have to take a risk, a vertical risk. We need to respond to trust with trust. We need to respond to vulnerability with vulnerability. When we do that in God's direction, we can receive infinite rewards.

The Bible shows us its heroes in a very interesting light. It shows them as people who struggled to trust God. I find that very encouraging, because I struggle, too. Sometimes they put their lives on the line, threw caution to the wind, and trusted God completely. At other times, they did everything but trust.

Abraham, the first patriarch who appears in the book of Genesis, shows us such a saga. At one point, he trusted God enough to uproot his life and head off to an unknown land of promise. Later, however, he had a child with the servant girl Hagar because he couldn't see how God was going to fulfill His promise through his barren wife Sarah. Still later, Abraham showed an extraordinary trust by offering up to God his beloved, only son Isaac.

Sometimes we trust God; sometimes we don't. I wish I could always trust God completely, but I don't. That's why I find such comfort when I read the stories of the great men and women of the Bible. They are complete portraits of real human beings. They reach up, and they also stumble. They encounter revelations and run up against perplexities.

And yet God involved them in His marvelous plan of redemption. He used imperfect men and women to spread His perfect grace. And that tells me He can do the same for us today.

We may not always be trustworthy, but God is.

Genesis 27 shows us a dramatic story of people who stumbled when they should have trusted. Four family members failed to trust God at a critical point in their lives.

We have already met one of them on a mountaintop. At the tender age of sixteen, Isaac stretched trust to the outer limits on Mount Moriah. That story is told in Genesis 22. Now, in Genesis 27, Isaac is an old man nearing the end of his life.

Isaac had fathered twins, Esau and Jacob. Esau was the firstborn, by a hair. But God had declared that Jacob, the second-born, would be the one to receive the birthright. It was through Jacob that God would create a great nation and thus fulfill His promise to Abraham.

Isaac, however, in his heart of hearts, loved Esau more than Jacob. Isaac saw more of himself in this strong, adventurous son who loved to be out hunting game. Large, hairy, and of ruddy complexion, Esau had become an honest, straightforward young man.

Jacob, on the other hand, preferred staying around home tending sheep. He was his mother Rebekah's favorite. Much more thoughtful and sensitive than his brother, Jacob could also be dishonest and conniving at times. He was more interested in spiritual things than his brother was, but he also coveted the birthright and its privileges.

Isaac didn't like Jacob's dishonest, conniving attitude, so he decided to give the birthright to Esau, who was, technically, the firstborn. God had told Isaac that Jacob was better suited to carry out the promise, to lead the next generation in the building of a nation of faith. But Isaac allowed his own impulses to trump his trust in God's plan about the birthright.

This is how the journal of a lonely God tells the story: "When Isaac was old and his eyes were so weak that he could no longer see, he called for Esau his older son and said to him, 'My son.' 'Here I am,' he answered. Isaac said, 'I am now an old man and don't know the day of my death. Now then, get your weapons—your quiver and bow—and go out to the open country to hunt some wild game for me. Prepare me the kind of tasty food I like and bring it to me to eat, so that I may give you my blessing before I die' " (Genesis 27:1–4).

The birthright entailed special privileges that belonged to the firstborn male child in a family. Prominent among those privileges was a double portion of the estate as an inheritance. If a man had two sons, as did Isaac, his estate would be divided into three portions, and the older son would receive two. If there were three sons, the estate would be divided into four portions, and the oldest son would receive two.

The oldest son also usually received a special blessing from his father as the one who would formally continue the family line.

In Deuteronomy 21:15–17 we find a prohibition against a father playing favorites among his sons by giving the birthright to someone other than the firstborn. But in this special case, God had required that the birthright be given to the younger of the twins. Isaac knew what God wanted. But he just couldn't trust that it was for the best.

When my daughters were toddlers, washing their hair was always a problem. They would sit in the bathtub while I put shampoo on their hair. But then, as soon as I poured water on them to make a lather, they would tip their head down. The shampoo ran into their eyes and made them wince and cry.

I explained to each child that if she just looked straight up at me, she could avoid getting shampoo in her eyes. She would agree. But then, just when I started rinsing her hair, her fear would overcome her trust, and she would look down again.

More shampoo in the eyes. More tears.

All too often I respond to God in a very similar way. I know God is a good Father. I'm sure He loves me. I believe I should trust Him. But sometimes, in a difficult situation, I panic and turn my eyes away from Him. This never solves the problem; I just become more afraid, as the "shampoo" blinds me.

Even though my daughters knew I loved them, they had a hard time trusting me in an uncomfortable situation. I knew I could protect them, but convincing them of that wasn't easy, especially when all they could see was soapy water coming down. Their lack of trust disappointed me, but it hurt them more. They were the ones who got shampoo in their eyes.

I'm sure my lack of trust hurts God, but how much more does it hurt me?

Isaac surely knew that God loved him and that God loved both his boys. But something else got in the way of trust that day when an old man needed to give his final blessing. Isaac had been willing to risk everything for God when he was sixteen, but now his own likes and dislikes had stiffened, his own tendencies had hardened into habits.

And Esau surely knew about God's plan too. But he made no protest. Isaac's alternative sounded fine to him. So he became an accessory to his father's disobedience.

That's why Isaac sent Esau out hunting. And that's why Esau went. After a hearty meal, Isaac intended to bless this son and give him his inheritance. He would make Esau the head of the family. Surely God could build a great nation through this strong, straightforward young man.

The misstep of mistrust didn't end with Isaac however. It inspired the same among other members of his family. "Now Rebekah was listening as Isaac spoke to his son Esau. When Esau left for the open country to hunt game and bring it back, Rebekah said to her son Jacob, 'Look, I overheard your father say to your brother Esau, "Bring me some game and prepare me some tasty food to eat, so that I may give you my blessing in the presence of the LORD before I die." Now, my son, listen carefully and do what I tell you: Go out to the flock and bring me two choice young goats, so I can prepare some tasty food for your father, just the way he likes it. Then take it to your father to eat, so that he may give you his blessing before he dies' " (Genesis 27:5–10).

Wife and mother Rebekah was drawn into the circle of mistrust. She knew her beloved Jacob was supposed to get the birthright. And now that outcome seemed threatened. So she took matters into her own hands. She decided to trick her husband into following God's plan. Rebekah didn't trust God to take care of His own plan in His own time in His own way.

Jacob made no protest either. He could have refused to scheme against his father. He could have decided to let God be God. Instead, he concluded that God helps those who help themselves.

The truth is, the Bible teaches the opposite. God helps those who realize they *can't* help themselves and who humbly trust God to be Lord in their lives.

The melodrama of Isaac and Rebekah, Esau and Jacob, spotlights an important principle: To be trusted is a greater compliment than to be loved.

Trust was a scarce commodity that day around the tents of Isaac. Mom and Dad were working behind each other's backs, scheming to make their respective favorites come out on top. And the two brothers, always rivals to a certain degree, had been sucked into the plots. Talk about a dysfunctional family!

At the root of the dysfunction lay each person's failure to trust God. This was the family destined to give birth to Israel. This was the family chosen to spread God's light to the world. But they were stuck at stage one: an inability to trust.

As it turned out, Rebekah and Jacob were successful in their scheme to deceive Isaac. The old man was legally blind. When Jacob slipped into his father's tent with food for him to eat, Isaac recognized the voice as that of Jacob. But when Jacob stepped closer, he smelled like Esau—because he was wearing Esau's clothes. And he felt like Esau—because he had wrapped hairy goat skin around his smooth arms.

So, Isaac believed it was Esau come back from the hunt, and he delivered his special blessing and transferred the birthright to Jacob.

But, of course, it wasn't long before the real Esau walked into his father's tent seeking the rights of a firstborn. His father was stunned. "Isaac trembled violently and said, 'Who was it, then, that hunted game and brought it to me? I ate it just before you came and I blessed him—and indeed he will be blessed!' " (Genesis 27:33).

The blessing couldn't be unsaid. The birthright couldn't be taken back. And the deception couldn't be undone. Isaac's heart broke when he learned his own family had betrayed him. Esau expressed dismay. "When Esau heard his father's words, he burst out with a loud and bitter cry and said to his father, 'Bless me—me too, my father!' " (Genesis 27:34).

The two men wept together, hurt and angry, lost in the shadows of a family torn apart. That's what lies on the other side of mistrust. It's a landscape of disaster.

After drying his tears, Esau swore that as soon as his father died, he would kill his brother. Rebekah learned of Esau's plan and warned Jacob. So Jacob fled. He traveled back to the land of Chaldea, the land Abraham had once left, planning to stay with relatives there.

It was a long, difficult journey that gave Jacob a lot of time to think. He thought about his life, about his relationships, about his family, and about his God. It seems that Jacob had to face some hard truths about himself, about what lay behind his deception. His troubled thoughts even invaded his sleep.

This young fugitive had a vivid dream. He saw a stairway reaching all the way to heaven. On the stairway angels appeared, God's messengers ascending and descending, faithfully carrying out His commands. The contrast between the angels' trusting obedience and his own distrust was surely not lost on Jacob.

At the top of the stairway stood the Almighty Himself. Genesis 28:13 tells us God made an announcement: " 'I am the LORD, the God of your father Abraham and the God of Isaac.' "

There was an important message about God's sovereignty behind this statement. God was saying, in effect, "Jacob, you are not God. I am God. I always have been God, and I always will be God. The sooner you figure that out and begin to trust Me, the better."

But God also had a promise to make. It was an expression of confidence in this broken, troubled young man. And it was also an inducement for Jacob to begin leaning on God instead of just himself. "I will give you and your descendants the land on which you are lying. Your descendants will be like the dust of the earth, and you will spread out to the west and to the east, to the north and to the south. All peoples on earth will be blessed through you and your offspring. I am with you and will watch over you wherever you go, and I will bring you back to this land. I will not leave you until I have done what I have promised you" (Genesis 28:13–15).

Jacob had failed miserably. He had lied and deceived his father and his brother.

He had stolen the birthright blessing God had promised to give him. But in the aftermath of this mess, God still had promises up His sleeve. God still had plans.

When God intercepted Jacob's flight from Canaan to Chaldea, He didn't just come with a rebuke. He didn't just put Jacob down. True, God confronted Jacob. But He did it with gentleness and grace. He enticed His wayward son with a great promise. He wooed him with a noble purpose.

The bottom line is that God trusted Jacob more than Jacob trusted God. God paid Jacob the ultimate compliment. Remember, to be trusted is a greater compliment than to be loved. That's grace! Grace paved the way for Jacob to begin trusting again. God made Himself vulnerable in order to give this dishonest schemer a second chance.

Well, it worked. Out there in the middle of nowhere, God got Jacob's attention. "Then Jacob made a vow, saying 'If God will be with me and will watch over me on this journey I am taking and will give me food to eat and clothes to wear so that I return safely to my father's house, then the LORD will be my God and this stone that I have set up as a pillar will be God's house, and of all that you give me I will give you a tenth' " (Genesis 28:20–22).

Finally, Jacob promised to let God be God. He decided to respond to God's reaching out by reaching back—with trust and obedience. And as a gesture of gratitude, he decided to give back to God a tenth of all his increase.

Jacob didn't become perfect overnight. He would struggle with trust issues the rest of his life. But he was a more secure human being now. And he began a more intimate, honest relationship with God that would become a legacy for generations to come.

Grace shines through this story in more ways than one. It spotlights the fact that God used a messy, dysfunctional family to accomplish His purposes. The Messiah would come through this family. Faith would be preserved through it. It would become a blessing for all humankind. And all this happened because just one person turned back in faith. One person began to trust.

God can use small gestures to reverse generations of mistrust. His grace knows no boundaries. He can do great things through flickers of faith in a dark landscape.

Ralph Waldo Emerson wrote, "All I have seen teaches me to trust the Creator for all I have not seen." The more we depend on God, the more dependable we find Him to be. Your life may be a mess. Your family may be a mess. But God has promises up His sleeve—just for you. No matter how dark your circumstances, trust can lead you to a better place. And remember, the highest pinnacle of the spiritual life is not joy in unbroken sunshine, but absolute trust in the love of God.

A. W. Tozer wrote, "What we need very badly these days is a company of Christians who are prepared to trust God as completely now as they know they must do at the last day. For each of us the time is coming when we shall have nothing but God. Health and wealth and friends and hiding places will be swept away, and we shall have only God. To the man of pseudo faith that is a terrifying thought, but to real faith it is one of the most comforting thoughts the heart can entertain."

God is looking for people who will pay Him the ultimate compliment by placing their trust completely in Him. He is looking for a people who will trust Him in good times and in bad times. He is looking for people who will trust Him enough to obey Him. When God finds such people, He rewards them with an intimate relationship that fulfills the deepest desires of their hearts. That kind of relationship will change you forever.

Three long years of captivity had worn down the inmates of Kampili, a notorious women's prison camp the Japanese had set up after their conquest of the Celebes islands. World War II dragged on and on. Many of the internees had become completely demoralized; most had grown apathetic; even the children there became listless. Rainy days thumped out an endless monotony.

One prisoner, however, a former missionary to New Guinea named Darlene Deibler Rose, responded to the crisis by reaching out in trust. She decided to pray.

Darlene petitioned the Lord on behalf of Mr. Yamaji, the brutal camp commander who would beat prisoners unmercifully when angered. One day, standing before him in his office, she had the opportunity to share a few words about the Almighty Creator who died for him. Tears ran down his cheeks, and he rushed into an adjoining room. After that day, Mr. Yamaji began to show kindness to her and even tried to improve camp conditions for everyone.

Darlene could very easily have let the unending disaster of imprisonment overshadow her faith. She could have doubted God had any meaningful plan for her life there in Kampili. Instead she concentrated on stretching her faith in the here and now. And so what stands out in this woman's recollections of that time were acts of Providence that lit up the long night like a flare gun.

One day Darlene was called into the hospital where Rachel, a Jewish internee, lay gasping for breath, trying to fight off a serious asthma attack. Darlene knelt by the bed and whispered, "Rachel, we pray to the same God. I'm going to pray for you now." The woman nodded; Darlene asked God to touch her body. Immediately her breathing eased, and the following morning Rachel returned to the barracks.

When the dreaded Kempeitai secret police took her to their prison, Darlene remembered to pray in faith. Her main request was that she might stand firm for Christ. As she prayed, she later said, "Strength came. God gave me the courage to deport myself like a good soldier for my Lord before those cruel men."

Because Darlene kept looking for signs of God's presence in that place, she found them. She saw God's reassuring gestures in the midst of disaster. One night she watched from her cell window as someone sneaked a bunch of bananas through a vine-covered fence to one of the native prisoners. Darlene dropped to the floor trembling, overcome by a craving. "Lord," she exclaimed, "just one banana!" A little later she gave thanks contritely for her rice porridge. But the next morning a guard walked into her cell and dropped a large cluster of bananas at her feet.

Darlene slowly counted ninety-two of the precious fruit and heard God whisper, "That's what I delight to do—the exceeding abundant above anything you ask or think."

Back at the compound, huddling with the other prisoners in huts because many barracks had been destroyed during weeks of air raids, Darlene prayed, "Please Lord, for the sake of the children, let there be no air raid tonight. There's no moon, and we don't know this area, so where would we hide?" The planes didn't come.

The Almighty was real and present for Darlene Deibler Rose in a place where He could have seemed agonizingly distant. She found Him in the here and now because she trusted. Although Darlene longed for the end of the war as fervently as anyone, she refused to confine her hopes and prayers to that day of final deliverance. Her prison life was not dominated by disaster, but propelled forward by two things—a continual endeavor to remain close to God through thick and thin and a continual awareness of His small favors.

As a result of Darlene's willingness to risk herself in trust, she was rewarded with a wonderfully intimate relationship with God. This was a woman who could look up at the stars from a bomb-blackened shelter and rejoice that the Creator of the heavens had become her Companion: "Oh, the wonder of His love for me and His personal concern for me, as an individual, was overwhelming," she testified later.

Centuries ago, God made a promise to Jacob, and today He repeats that same promise to you: "I am with you and will watch over you wherever you go" (Genesis 28:15).

God extends such great promises toward us. The quality of our life will be determined by how wholeheartedly we grasp them as gifts from a Father who has earned our trust.

Wrestling With God

GENESIS 32

Oscar Wilde wrote, "In this world there are only two tragedies. One is not getting what one wants, and the other is getting it." I would suggest there are two joys in this world. One is having God answer all your prayers; the other is *not* receiving the answers you ask for. It has taken me a long time to come to this conclusion. But I have seen over and over that God knows my needs infinitely better than I do. And sometimes *not* getting what I pray for is precisely what I need.

It took Jacob a long time to come to the same conclusion. The lessons he had to learn were painful, but invaluable. A lonely God wanted the very best for Jacob. He wanted to develop in this man a capacity for spiritual intimacy. And God knew Jacob would have to go through some pretty tough experiences in order to get there.

Jacob would have to learn to give up, to surrender himself and his will to God. He would have to experience brokenness. He would have to let go of what he wanted in order to grasp what God wanted for him.

All Jacob ever wanted, after all, was—everything! He wanted to be firstborn, instead of second. He wanted his brother Esau's birthright. He determined to marry a beauty queen—not the spinster sister with which he found himself. He wanted to be rich and prosperous—like Uncle Laban who kept going back on his promises. Jacob thought he should have an easy life. But he ended up knee-deep in strife.

Jacob's struggles began before he was even born. His mother Rebekah, while carrying twins, said she could feel her two boys fighting even in the womb.

After Esau emerged with loud cries, Rebekah asked her midwife, "Can you see the second one yet?"

The midwife replied "The firstborn isn't quite the firstborn yet."

A grimacing Rebekah asked how this could be.

"He's hung up by one foot," the midwife explained. "I don't ever remember such a sight. The second born is holding his brother by the foot, as if he's trying to pull him back in."

The midwife knew this was a bad omen. Any child born hand-first, instead of headfirst, couldn't amount to much. Rebekah named him Jacob, which means "Heel Grabber." The firstborn was named Esau, or "Big Red."

Jacob and Esau were anything but identical twins. Esau grew up thinking of Jacob as a mama's boy. And Jacob thought his brother a bit of a brute. Their rivalry culminated in that terrible deception—Jacob stealing the birthright right under the nose of his blind old father. Esau making violent threats. Jacob fleeing to the land of his ancestors.

That's why Heel Grabber walked up to the tents of a man named Laban one day and offered his services. He wanted to make a new start there with his uncle, his mother Rebekah's brother. Laban looked over his nephew and decided he might prove quite useful. In Laban, a scheming Jacob had met his match.

Laban had two daughters. Rachel was a lovely girl; every young shepherd within a hundred miles had an eye out for Rachel. Her sister, Leah, was not so fortunate. Her looks weren't going to win her much of a dowry.

Jacob fell hard for Rachel, and Laban talked him into a seven-year deal. If Jacob worked for Laban faithfully for seven years, he could marry the girl. The time flew by because love was in the air. But on the night of his wedding, when it was finally time to unveil the bride, Jacob discovered he had just married Leah! Uncle Laban had originated the bait-and-switch move.

Incredibly enough, smitten Jacob agreed to work seven more years for the woman he actually wanted as his wife. If this wedding had been delayed to the end of the contract, he and Rachel would be saying vows in midlife. So Jacob insisted on marrying her first and then putting in another seven years.

At the end of this fourteen-year contract, Jacob still felt resentful over Laban's wife swindle. So he rustled a herd of his uncle's livestock, placed the equivalent of his brand on them, and took off under cover of night.

Jacob was headed home. He was headed home to confront the shadows of his past and, hopefully, a brighter future. Days into his journey, he came to a brook named Jabbok and set up camp for the night. And there, out under the stars, Jacob finally had a face-to-face encounter with God. In a sense he was finally climbing up that ladder he'd seen many years before.

"Then Jacob was left alone; and a Man wrestled with him until the breaking of day. Now when He saw that He did not prevail against him, He touched the socket of his hip; and the socket of Jacob's hip was out of joint as He wrestled with him. And He said, 'Let Me go, for the day breaks.' But he said, 'I will not let You go unless You bless me!' " (Genesis 32:24–26, NKJV).

Jacob wasn't wrestling with an ordinary adversary. He was facing off against supernatural strength. But then he'd always been a headstrong individual; he'd gone to great lengths to get his own way. And it took quite a big struggle for him to submit to someone bigger than himself, to God.

The amazing thing is that God was willing to get "down and dirty" in order to help Jacob through his crisis of faith. He didn't strike this man down for his presumption. The heart of a lonely God would not allow that. If having a close relationship with Jacob meant wrestling in the wee hours of the morning, then that's what He would do.

If you're a dad, I'm sure you've wrestled with your children. When they're small, they love to jump on your back and make a lot of noise and act as if they're taking you down. You weigh two hundred pounds. They're thirty-five pounds after a good supper. They have about as much chance of beating you as I do of slamming the professional wrestler, the Rock. But you still have a great wrestling match.

God the Father allows His children to wrestle with Him. He allows us to shove our perplexities and disappointments and anger and demands right in His face. The odds of winning a wrestling match with God are not great, of course. But we try all the time. For example, we may know what God wants; we can read His directives in black and white, but we still resist. We keep insisting there has to be an alternative. We keep fighting to get our own way.

Any time He wants, God could just flex a muscle and send us flying. He could body slam all of our petulant questions, all of our indignation, all of our presumption. But He doesn't. Instead He allows us to pound on His chest and cry out against the dark and flail against reality. God doesn't need to win the match. He allows us to struggle until we run out of energy.

Jacob was the kind of person who wanted everything and wanted it now. He didn't want to give in to God. But God's plans were so much better than anything he could come up with, and Jacob needed to acknowledge that.

So God did something to halt Jacob's headlong rush from one disaster to another. He touched Jacob's hip, and it came out of joint. That got his attention. He stopped wrestling, and he started pleading. Crippled for the moment, Jacob asked for God's will to become a reality in his life. It was through being maimed that Jacob finally gave up on his dreams of "having it all." Only then did he experience the brokenness of spirit that opens each of us up to divine blessing.

I've seen that principle play out in my own life. I can be pretty stubborn. I've latched on to certain goals, certain things I want—and hung on for dear life. In my heart of hearts I'm determined to have my own way. I've wrestled with God, not just all night, but for weeks, months, and even years!

When you've got your heart set on a prize, you can fight a long time. I remember times when I've cried out to God long and hard—trying to get my way. I've begged for a blessing—not just any blessing but the blessing I want in the way I want it.

But God knows best for me, and eventually I receive the equivalent of a dislocated hip. I'm immobilized. I run out of options. I feel overwhelmed by circumstances. And finally I wake up to reality and what I need to do. I need to submit to God and accept His will for my life.

It's only when I experience brokenness of spirit in some way that I'm able to really listen to God and receive all that He wants to give me. As long as I believe I can still somehow manipulate things to go my way, still somehow use my own strength to get away with something, then the answers elude me. And what's more, genuine closeness with Christ slips away too.

Brokenness has often preceded blessing in my life. It's a painful experience. It's not something too many of us would volunteer for. But it's the door to better things. For someone as stubborn as I am, the state of limping around and nursing my wounds isn't a bad place to be. That's what leads me to genuine surrender and obedience.

Jacob walked away from the brook Jabbok with a limp. His hip didn't heal perfectly. But that wound would precede a great breakthrough into blessing. That brokenness would make Jacob obedient. And it would lead to reconciliation with his brother Esau.

Have you wrestled with God? How many matches have you gone through with the King of kings? How many more will you experience before you're through?

I was a young man when I came to my own Jabbok. I had sensed a call to ministry ever since I was a boy, ever since I could remember. But as I stumbled through my teenage years, I began to rebel against that call.

I wanted an easier life, for one thing. I wanted shorter hours, better pay, and more vacation time. So I decided to major in business. Why not try to make a bundle? I didn't make it through too many business classes, however. Nothing clicked. This wasn't what I was supposed to pursue. So I decided to move a bit closer to the area God had spotlighted for me. I switched to education and music. That was kind of similar to church work; it was in the same ballpark, at least.

Looking back, I can see that I was negotiating. I was trying to bargain with God. *Surely education and music is good enough. What's more, I won't just teach,*

I'll teach history and religion. Surely that should satisfy the big plan. Maybe it's not exactly what God wants, but it's close.

It was a prolonged wrestling match, and I was fighting for a draw. In college I'd given up actually winning the fight, but thought maybe I wouldn't have to lose either.

After graduation I taught school for some time and completed a degree in counseling. It seemed that I was making a pretty good life for myself and raising a good family. But the wrestling match continued.

One day I received a ministerial license in the mail. I was teaching at a Christian school, and the license came from the state organization of the church that was sponsoring the school. Now, this kind of thing simply was not done. This church didn't just mail out licenses like that. But it happened in my case.

Still, I wasn't seeking a formal acceptance into the gospel ministry. I continued teaching. But one summer, church leaders said they would like to ordain me as a minister. Quite surprised, I accepted.

But I hadn't given up yet. I decided to quit teaching and go into business with my parents. This kept me quite busy, of course. But wouldn't you know it, someone called and asked me to serve as interim pastor of a church. This person explained it was only a part-time position; I could continue doing my business. Anyway, it was only a six-week assignment, so I accepted.

That assignment lasted seven and a half years. The cold water of the brook Jabbok was rising fast. It was coming up over my knees. I felt as if God was saying, "Still not convinced? How about two out of three falls?"

The bell rang; I wrestled with God as long as I could. He put moves on me that I thought were illegal. And in the end He had me on the mat. I admitted that He'd won the match. I admitted where I belonged. And to make a long story short, I have found the greatest fulfillment in serving as a pastor.

I wanted an easy life; God wanted the best life. I wanted shortcuts; God wanted to give me the blessing that comes through brokenness.

There's a sense in which I limp to this day. But there's also a sense in which it feels good when God hurts you. He opens up a life that's truly abundant.

Do you find yourself wrestling with God today? What will it take for you to acknowledge, from your heart, that He must be the winner? The truth is, the only way for us to win in life is to lose to God. We have to give up. That's how we come out on top in the fight. When we submit our entire lives to His will, we ensure ourselves genuine success. We win a life of meaning, fulfillment, peace, happiness, purpose, and joy.

Some folks are smart enough to give up the wrestling match while the night is still young. They get a good night's rest. But others of us are not so smart. We stubbornly wrestle on into the night, until God finally cripples us. That's the only way we will ever learn to be dependent on Him.

You know, by most accounts, sheep are among the dumbest animals on earth. And they're completely defenseless. When an enemy approaches, there's not much they can do. Their eyesight and hearing are not good enough to spot trouble from a distance. They're not fast enough to outrun a coyote or a mountain lion. They don't have sharp teeth or claws with which to stand and fight. And they don't have the smarts to find a place of safety.

Without a shepherd to watch their every move, sheep just don't last very long. The ones most at risk are those who combine stupidity with stubbornness. They get it into their modest little brains that they can manage just fine on their own. They don't need the flock. They don't need the shepherd. And they develop a nasty habit of wandering off by themselves.

A shepherd has to keep a sharp eye out for those wayward lambs. He guides them back to the flock as soon as they start to wander. Sometimes he may have to use his shepherd's rod to correct a persistent wanderer, whacking it on the side so it will obey. And if the lamb still doesn't respond, the shepherd sometimes must resort to desperate measures. He does the unthinkable. He breaks that little lamb's leg. Then he sets it.

It's painful, and it's ugly. But during the time this lamb is healing, the shepherd carries it everywhere. It can only hobble around and tires quite easily. It can't make it across rocky ground or streams. So it spends much of the day under the shepherd's arm or across his shoulders.

By the time the leg has mended, the lamb has bonded with the shepherd. It has learned its lesson. It never loses sight of him and will always stay with his flock. And so the lamb that was doomed because it just had to wander will survive and thrive in the shepherd's care.

A lot of us have a tendency to wander. We know where we're supposed to be headed, but something else catches our eye and we just have to set off after it. Our Good Shepherd calls out to us. He tries to keep us close. He nudges us back toward the flock. When we don't respond to His voice, He sometimes has to use His sturdy rod. But some of us just ignore the pain and press on with our plans.

The fight rages on until, in desperation, the Shepherd allows something to cripple us. We run into an obstacle that breaks our will. It pains the heart of a lonely God, but He wants to do everything He can to keep us from the cliff.

Something terrible may have happened in your life, and you keep wondering why God would allow such a thing. If He's so all-powerful, if He's so loving, why would He just stand there as this calamity unfolds? Well, how about looking at the bigger picture? Did that calamity come after a long wrestling match? Was that calamity a way to dislocate your hip and stop your struggle? Could it be that you need to learn to depend on God completely even more than you need release from the thing that's hurting you?

We want an easy life. It's a natural, human instinct. And usually it keeps us from unnecessary trouble and pain. But sometimes that instinct turns into a stubborn resolve to have it our way, period, and to fight anything that threatens our plans.

And that's when our Good Shepherd has to apply some tough love. He's willing to use the painful things, the ugly things that happen in this sinful world, for our benefit. The tonic may be hard to swallow. But there's healing on the other side.

Part of the pastoral responsibilities that I carry out each week at my church is to serve as a counselor. Counselors specialize in conflict resolution. When parents are caught up in unresolved conflicts with their teenagers, for example, I help both sides realize the value of give-and-take.

Compromise can lead to reconciliation. Both parties give a little, and both parties get a little for the sake of peace.

The same dynamic holds true in marriage counseling. Unhappy spouses usually want something from their marriage that they simply aren't getting. The counselor often has to teach both parties how to negotiate more fairly and openly. If you give a little here, you can gain a little there. The hallmark of successful counseling is to help people find win-win solutions. And that usually revolves around compromise.

But conflicts with God are very different. That's what Jacob discovered at Jabbok. He was a man who wanted it all: security, wealth, the blessing, the birthright, and the beauty queen for a wife. When he realized he might lose it all, Jacob tried to negotiate. He was willing to compromise. He was telling God, "I'll just give a little over here, and You can give me a little over there!"

But in the middle of that dark night, struggling against his unyielding adversary, Jacob found that God isn't into compromise. God is into surrender. God gets you into a win-win situation by taking you through a lose-lose experience.

What do you want out of life? What are your non-negotiable points? If you're like most of us, your tastes are very simple. You want just one thing: the best! And you don't want to have to sacrifice an arm and a leg to get it.

But God often has a very different picture of "the best." And sometimes we do lose an arm or a leg. Sometimes we do have to give up on long-held dreams or cherished plans or our vision of the good life. Sometimes God breaks our hearts in order to heal them.

Maybe you wonder why an Almighty God has to use such strong medicine. Shouldn't there be an easier way? Just remember Jesus wondered the same thing in Gethsemane. Wasn't there some way to rescue the world from sin without having all hell break loose inside Him?

The answer was no. The Son of God had to give Himself up completely and be consumed by our calamity. And God the Father had to give up His Son. He had to let Him die alone on Calvary.

Jesus doesn't just *tell* us what we must do to break through to God's blessing. He *shows* us what we must do. Jesus surrendered. Jesus surrendered heart, body, and soul. And as a result, He crafted a win-win solution for all of humanity.

If Jesus needed to surrender to God, you need to surrender too. It's the only way to win. It's far better than getting it all. It's the way to get eternal life.

We can get to that coveted place the easy way, or we can get there the hard way. We can surrender our will to God at sunset and get a good night's rest, or we can fight on through the night and not give up until the sun rises.

The first option is far better. I should know. I walk with a limp.

Joseph: Faithful Young Man

GENESIS 37–39

Throughout the centuries, a lonely God has searched for people who would be receptive to a relationship of intimacy. Often the most receptive are the very young.

We saw an example of that in the story of sixteen-year-old Isaac who trusted God so much he was willing to lay down on a mountaintop altar while his father prepared to offer him as a sacrifice.

Later, a six-year-old boy named Samuel would find a role in Jerusalem's temple. In a time when few among the chosen were paying much attention to God's voice, this child listened. God awakened him one night and delivered an important message for the high priest Eli, which the boy faithfully delivered. Samuel became the focal point of God's plans for the Hebrew nation.

A shepherd boy and composer of psalms named David walked out on the field of battle one day and, in the name of the God of heaven, challenged a Philistine giant. Seasoned soldiers all around him stood paralyzed by fear. But this lad, moved by a confidence in the Almighty's power, gathered five smooth stones for his sling and walked straight toward Goliath.

A long period of spiritual decline in Judah was interrupted when an eight-year-old child named Josiah became king. He determined to do what was "right in the eyes of the Lord." The youthful sovereign ordered that the temple, which had been neglected and had fallen into disrepair, be restored. After discovering a copy of the Law of Moses there, Josiah led the nation in a great revival, restoring their covenant relationship with the God of heaven.

Over and over, a lonely God finds kindred spirits among the young in spirit. Youthful men and women prove the most receptive to His invitations.

Joash was just seven when he began to reign in Jerusalem. Like Samuel, he listened to the voice of God and obeyed. Like Josiah, he restored the temple and led a national revival.

Daniel and his three friends were teenagers when they were taken from their homes and exiled to far-off Babylon. But they stood tall for their faith, refusing to conform to the customs of that idolatrous land.

It's a phenomenon spotlighted in the narrative of Scripture. Young people show themselves receptive to the voice of God when others have grown deaf. Their tender hearts take them on great adventures with Him.

Later in life, people tend to shrink into complacency and cynicism. They develop spiritual inertia. Today we have statistics to point this out. If people do not accept Christ while still in their youth, the chances that they will experience a conversion diminish dramatically as they get older.

The younger years are critical years. They are filled with more spiritual potential than most of us realize. In the journal of a lonely God, a boy named Joseph fleshes out this theme. His story begins in Genesis 37. "This is the account of Jacob. Joseph, a young man of seventeen, was tending the flocks with his brothers, the sons of Bilhah and the sons of Zilpah, his father's wives, and he brought their father a bad report about them" (Genesis 37:2).

Remember that Jacob had first married Leah, and then Rachel, the woman he really loved. Eventually he also took their respective handmaidens—Bilhah and Zilpah—as his wives. Jacob fathered twelve sons by these four women.

But he had a special regard for two of the youngest boys, Joseph and Benjamin. Their mother was his beloved Rachel. And Jacob would discover what his grandfather Abraham had learned many years earlier. Marrying more than one woman is an invitation to family dysfunction.

The four wives nursed twelve sons and also kept jealousies and resentments well fed. Their quarrels were fueled by the fact that Jacob could not conceal his favoritism. Their children grew up in a melodrama, shaped to a great extent by the animosity circulating around the tents of Jacob.

One day, when the fighting among half-brothers got a bit out of hand, Joseph told on them. He brought a "bad report" to father Jacob. There was already bad blood between him and his half-brothers. And this only made it worse. His mother had always been the favorite wife. Now Joseph had become the favorite son.

Now Israel loved Joseph more than any of his other sons, because he had been born to him in his old age; and he made a richly ornamented robe for him. When his brothers saw that their father loved him more than any of them, they hated him and could not speak a kind word to him.

Joseph had a dream, and when he told it to his brothers, they hated him all the more. He said to them, "Listen to this dream I had: We were binding sheaves of grain out in the field when suddenly my sheaf rose and stood upright, while your sheaves gathered around mine and bowed down to it."

JOSEPH: FAITHFUL YOUNG MAN

His brothers said to him, "Do you intend to reign over us? Will you actually rule us?" And they hated him all the more because of his dream and what he had said (Genesis 37:3–8).

Joseph was naïve to be sure. He didn't know when to keep things to himself. None of his half-brothers had any inclination to bow down to this little brat. So, of course, his cheerful sharing of the dream only intensified their hatred.

But there was something besides Joseph's innocence at work here. His dream wasn't just a random event or the product of childish fantasies. It was a prophecy. It was a divine glimpse of the future. And the fact that Joseph took it in and immediately shared it with others suggests his heart was open to God. He didn't fully understand what this unusual dream meant. But he was willing to listen and respond.

Unfortunately, however, Joseph wasn't a good diplomat. He didn't understand how he was fueling resentment. The boy had a second dream, which he immediately and unthinkingly shared with everyone:

Then he had another dream, and he told it to his brothers. "Listen," he said, "I had another dream, and this time the sun and moon and eleven stars were bowing down to me."

When he told his father as well as his brothers, his father rebuked him and said, "What is this dream you had? Will your mother and I and your brothers actually come and bow down to the ground before you?" His brothers were jealous of him, but his father kept the matter in mind (Genesis 37:9–11).

Joseph was too young to have developed sophisticated social skills. He didn't know how to play politics. He just knew that God seemed to be giving him a message.

One day, Jacob sent Joseph to check up on his sons who were grazing sheep in a distant pasture. These half-brothers could see him coming a long way off in the flat grassland, and they weren't happy about it. There was Daddy's little dreamer again, probably come to spy on them and report back to Jacob. They began talking about how annoying he was. Someone surely reminded them that this kid had been chosen to receive the birthright. He would get double the inheritance of anyone else.

The more these ten sons of Jacob talked, the angrier they got. Finally they decided to solve this problem once and for all. "But they saw him in the distance, and before he reached them, they plotted to kill him. 'Here comes that dreamer!' they said to each other. 'Come now, let's kill him and throw him into one of these cisterns and say that a ferocious animal devoured him. Then we'll see what comes of his dreams' " (Genesis 37:18–20).

This terrible plot had actually been hatching for a long time. It had its roots in generations past. Jacob himself had been part of the family's dysfunction. Two parents, Isaac and Rebekah, tried to maneuver their respective favorite sons for advantage. Rivalry and jealousy had torn Jacob apart from his brother and father. Playing favorites was the only way he knew to do family. And so all the animosity associated with his dysfunction was passed on to the next generation.

It boiled over in that pastureland under a hot midday sun. Jacob's sons had nursed their grudge until it hardened into a murderous intent. But one brother realized how horrible this crime really was. "When Reuben heard this, he tried to rescue him [Joseph] from their hands. 'Let's not take his life,' he said. 'Don't shed any blood. Throw him into this cistern here in the desert, but don't lay a hand on him.' Reuben said this to rescue him from them and take him back to his father" (Genesis 37:21, 22).

The boys agreed. As soon as Joseph walked up with a cheery greeting, they deposited him in the bottom of a dry well. Later, while Reuben was away checking on the sheep, a caravan came by, which gave them an idea. Why not make a nice profit from this pain-in-the-neck dreamer? So they sold Joseph as a slave to a caravan bound for Egypt. Then they dipped his many colored coat in blood and took it back home to Jacob, telling him their brother must have been attacked by a wild animal.

Joseph became a slave in the house of Potiphar, an official in Pharaoh's government. He was a long, long way from his nice, warm place as the favorite son of the favorite wife. His innocence had been torn from him. This broken young man had every reason in the world to give up. It would have been so easy to conclude that those dreams were just a cruel joke. It would have been easy to believe that God played favorites too, and he was not one of them.

But Joseph somehow kept clinging to the faith of his childhood. He kept believing that God still had a plan—even in exile, lost from his family, captive in a heathen land. As time passed, Joseph distinguished himself in the service of Potiphar. He worked so cheerfully and efficiently that Potiphar placed him in charge of his entire household. Everything entrusted to Joseph just seemed to prosper. Genesis tells us that "The LORD blessed the household of the Egyptian because of Joseph. The blessing of the LORD was on everything Potiphar had, both in the house and in the field" (Genesis 39:5).

Joseph took care of the cattle and the farmland. Joseph maintained Potiphar's estate in good working order. Joseph managed the servants and the finances. And because of God's blessing, he seemed to do everything well.

But then Potiphar's wife started taking notice. "Now Joseph was well-built and handsome, and after a while his master's wife took notice of Joseph and said, 'Come to bed with me!'" (Genesis 39:6, 7).

It is very likely that Potiphar was gone on government business quite a lot. So Mrs. Potiphar had her listless days and lonely nights. Joseph had grown up on a sheep ranch in the middle of nowhere. The only women he knew were his father's wives, a few sisters, and a few servants. In his culture, women were taught to be quiet and demure. They were clothed in garments that covered everything but their eyes, hands, and feet.

But these Egyptian women were something else! They didn't dress as modestly, and they weren't afraid to flirt. And now the beautiful, confident woman of the house was coming on to him. For a healthy young man, this was no easy temptation to resist. Joseph did manage to politely decline. The problem was, he had to keep doing it. "And though she spoke to Joseph day after day, he refused to go to bed with her or even be with her" (Genesis 39:10).

Joseph tried to avoid the woman as much as he could. But she kept finding ways for the two of them to be alone. Joseph found himself in an extremely vulnerable position. This woman had all the power, all the authority over him. And he had to keep saying "No." What's more, he had to try to avoid thinking about her, fantasizing about her.

Just when he thought he couldn't stand it any longer, it got worse. "One day he went into the house to attend to his duties, and none of the household servants was inside. She caught him by his cloak and said, 'Come to bed with me!' But he left his cloak in her hand and ran out of the house" (Genesis 39:11, 12).

Joseph did something you will never see any leading man do on the big screen. He turned away from a sure thing. Faced with an overwhelming temptation, Joseph ran away from the temptress. He would not betray the man who had entrusted everything into his care. She was clutching his cloak. She wasn't going to take no for an answer. But Joseph left it in her hands. And that proved to be the undoing of this honest young man.

Mrs. Potiphar accused Joseph of attacking her. Hell has no fury like a woman scorned, and this woman had power along with her fury. It is likely that Potiphar trusted Joseph more than he trusted his wife because he knew them both well. But he would lose face before his entire household if word got out that his wife had tried to seduce a servant. So he had Joseph thrown into a dungeon.

Joseph paid a high price for faithfulness to God. But he had developed a habit of listening and obeying. He had responded when God inspired him to dream great things. And he wasn't going to turn his back when God took him through a time of trouble. Relationships are about going through the good times and the bad times together.

There in a wealthy Egyptian estate, surrounded by emblems of Pharaoh worship, God found a young person who wanted to be His friend. And eventually God would find a way to lift His friend out of the dungeon and up to the heights of Egyptian power as Pharaoh's viceroy.

I hear a lot of talk today about young people. It's typical for every generation to worry aloud about the next. Older Christians who are established in the faith see few signs of hope in the younger crowd: "There's so much promiscuity and drugs and partying out there. And the kids look pretty scary. Look at all the body parts they're piercing these days." So young people get written off.

Well, guess what? When we were their age, the older folk said exactly the same thing about us. We had our own ways of scaring our parents to death. In order to forge their own identities, most self-respecting teenagers feel compelled to come up with a style of music or clothing that freaks out their parents.

But you know, as a pastor I've counseled with plenty of young people and plenty of adults. And I find that neither group has a corner on sin. Human weaknesses plague us all. The only difference I consistently observe between the two groups is that younger people tend to be more receptive when I talk about their problems. They are less defensive and less cynical. They seem more tender toward the impressions of the Holy Spirit.

I'm not afraid to talk to our kids honestly about the challenges they face. As long as a young person knows you love him and genuinely care, he will listen when you talk. But I've also found something else to be true. Many of these young people inspire me. I've discovered that a surprising number have taken stands like Joseph and Daniel and a host of other young luminaries from the Bible.

I believe in our kids! They aren't perfect. I know that better than most. But nothing encourages me more than to see kids who are struggling against enormous pressures and seemingly insurmountable odds remain faithful to Jesus.

Studies today indicate that we lose nearly 70 percent of our young people from the church on the day they graduate from high school. That is a heartbreaking number. It is a disgraceful number!

But there is another study that indicates something even more incredible.

This study shows that if just six adults in a church know a young person's first name and greet that young person on a regular basis, it's unlikely that young person will ever leave the church!

How many names of the kids in your church do you know? How many of these kids do you greet in the hallways by their first name? How many of them know that you know them—love them and care for them?

Do you want to do some evangelism? Learn the first name of just six kids and look for them every week. Greet them and engage them in conversation. Show them you care. You will be doing a more effective kind of evangelism than you can imagine.

But something else becomes apparent as you get involved in this way. You will discover that many of them are a lot like Joseph. They definitely have a heart for God; they listen to His voice, and they even make it their business to obey that voice.

In writing to a young man named Timothy, Paul told him he should not allow anyone to despise him for being young. That's a message for every young person in church. However awkward you may feel in church at times, God has a special place in His heart for people just like you. He feels a special affinity for the young. And He longs to form close relationships with you.

So I challenge youth today with this message: Now is the time. These are the good old days when you can form a lasting relationship with the God of Joseph, the God of heaven. Respond to Him today before you become jaded, before your innocence fades altogether. Have a heart for God; listen to His voice, and learn to obey Him. He is a Friend who will never put you down and will never let you down.

Let me tell you about a young man named Arthur who found himself wandering around Europe one summer, trying to figure out what life was all about. He hadn't seen all that much that was good in the world. He wasn't at all sure that God even existed.

But someone had given him a New Testament. Arthur was Jewish and not disposed to read that part of the Bible. He'd never really read the story in the Gospels. But since he was checking out all kinds of answers, he decided to give it a try.

One afternoon while on a ship crossing the Mediterranean, he started reading about Jesus. He sat in steerage, the crowded part of the ship. He held the New Testament while wedged among chickens, turkeys, babies, and passengers.

It was hard to concentrate at first. But as Arthur read, he couldn't help but become interested in this character Jesus. He seemed so different from any other religious figure he'd read about. Arthur came to the story of Jesus clashing with His religious rivals, the Pharisees, over a woman caught in adultery. He got caught up in the drama. The incident happened in the temple courtyard in Jerusalem. The Pharisees, the keepers of the Law, had dragged this woman before Jesus as He was teaching at the temple. They proclaimed loudly that they'd caught her in the act. There she was, sprawled before them, totally humiliated.

The Pharisees demanded to know what Jesus wanted done with the woman. Should they stone her to death, as the Old Testament Law decreed?

Arthur was reading this story in the Gospel of John, with all the noisy passengers around him. And he realized the Pharisees were trying to trap Jesus.

Arthur's pulse quickened. If Jesus said, "Don't stone the poor woman," He would appear to contradict the Law. If He said, "Go ahead and stone her," He would get in trouble with the Roman authorities. They were the only ones who could impose capital punishment.

Jesus was caught between a rock and a hard place. For a moment Arthur paused, wondering what Jesus could possibly say in return. Then he read these words, " 'If anyone of you is without sin, let him be the first to throw a stone at her' " (John 8:7).

Arthur gasped. What an extraordinary response! It had the ring of truth. Later, recalling his feelings at this moment, Arthur said, "A sword had been plunged deep into my being. It was numbing, shocking, yet thrilling because the answer was so utterly perfect. . . . It cut across every major issue I had ever anguished upon in my life. . . . I knew that what I had read transcended human knowledge and comprehension. It had to be divine."

Something remarkable had happened to Arthur on that ship in the Mediterranean. He wasn't just reading a book. He had come face to face with an extraordinary Person. He'd come face to face with Jesus. His young heart was listening. His young heart was ready to respond. And Arthur began a wonderful journey that day that ended in a wonderfully intimate relationship with God.

Wouldn't it be wonderful if each one of us could recover a young heart, a listening heart? Wouldn't it be wonderful if we could hear the good news as if for the first time? We need to recover the taste of a spiritual journey, a spiritual adventure.

Jesus made it a point to tell His mature hearers that none of us can enter into the kingdom of God unless we become like children. He longs for each of us to develop a special kind of youthfulness, a more responsive soul, a more trusting spirit. He wants each of us to taste the cheerful dependence of a child.

That's part of the miracle of grace. A new heart of flesh replaces our rigid hearts of stone. There's a way back to intimacy. It's a way opened up by the heart of a lonely God. A jaded mind can awaken to the wonder of knowing God face to face. And aching limbs can begin to chase a new dream and embark on a new journey of obedience, following God through the good times and the bad times, toward a glorious rendezvous in the heavens.

Lonely No Longer

GENESIS 46–50

In this book we've had the privilege of reading entries from the journal of the Creator God of the universe. We've seen something of His private thoughts and have begun to uncover what matters most to Him.

In counseling, I often ask people to tell me what their passion is, what they live for. It's an important question because it reveals a lot about who a person is. If you live for your children, then the "real you" is a mom or dad. That is who you are at your core.

If you would die for your spouse, then the "real you" is a husband or wife. If you would die for Jesus Christ, then the "real you" is His disciple.

Studying Genesis, this journal of a lonely God, has shown us God's greatest passion. We discovered who He is at the core of His being. And to our surprise, we've learned that what God lives for, and what He would die for is—us! Fallen men and women are the reason God lives from one day to the next. Sinful human beings are the reason God chose to die.

God Almighty simply wasn't completely fulfilled being alone, so He created universes and worlds inhabited by perfect beings who could choose to love Him and be loved by Him. But on one planet, disaster struck. Intelligent creatures turned away from that love. God knew their tragic choices would eventually lead to the annihilation of the human race. So He devised a plan to rescue us from that outcome. It was a plan that cost Him everything and cost us nothing.

When you get right down to it, God chose to make this sacrifice because He could not bear the thought of spending eternity without you. That's why He has invested so much in helping us understand the plan. The journal of a lonely God is a record of how this creating, redeeming God persuaded weak, selfish, distracted individuals to accept that plan and give themselves to it. It's the story of a God searching the world for men and women who might respond to the idea of an intimate relationship with their Creator.

Whenever God spotted some likely candidates for such a friendship, He gave Himself to them in amazing ways. He made wonderful promises. He talked them through their perplexities. He blessed their endeavors. He taught them invaluable lessons in their hardships and trials. At every turn this lonely God made available the kind of extravagant love that no person in their right mind would refuse. Unfortunately, a lot of us aren't quite in our right mind.

God loved Adam and Eve in a very special way as His firstborn children. But then we find He also loved Abraham and Sarah in a special way. And He loved Isaac and Jacob and Joseph in a special way. Pretty soon it becomes clear that this lonely God has an incredible capacity for love. His real plan is for everyone to become "the chosen."

The love of God for us is greater than we can understand or even imagine. But this much we can know for certain—a lonely God loves you too much to let you live alone, to let you die alone, or to leave you in the grave.

That becomes crystal clear in the final great drama of Genesis. In chapter 46 we pick up the story of the final days of Jacob. God had given this patriarch a new name—Israel. And the descendants of his twelve sons would eventually become the twelve tribes of Israel.

Jacob has heard wonderful news. His beloved son Joseph is alive and doing well in Egypt. He had grieved for his lost boy for twenty-two years. And now he's been invited to go and pay him a visit, daring to believe the tale his other sons have told him about this viceroy of Egypt.

"So Israel set out with all that was his, and when he reached Beersheba, he offered sacrifices to the God of his father Isaac. And God spoke to Israel in a vision at night and said, 'Jacob! Jacob!' 'Here I am,' he replied. 'I am God, the God of your father,' he said. 'Do not be afraid to go down to Egypt, for I will make you into a great nation there. I will go down to Egypt with you, and I will surely bring you back again. And Joseph's own hand will close your eyes' " (Genesis 46:1–4).

God understood the grief of His friend Israel. He knew all that was in his lonely heart. Grief is the loneliest work in the world. When you grieve, you feel as though no one understands, no one cares, no one knows the depth of your pain. Grief even makes God appear distant and unconcerned. Grief isolates.

But the God of Jacob found a way to break through that painful isolation. He gave His friend a vision to reassure him that he'd never really been alone. God had been with Jacob every step of the way.

And that's a message for everyone who has to go through the grieving process.

Your feelings, though very real, do not tell the whole story. They aren't the final word or the ultimate test of reality. As overwhelming as your sense of complete abandonment may be, it's not an accurate picture of your situation.

Because a lonely God is there with you. He feels the pain you feel. He cries every tear you cry. He experiences every pang of loss and loneliness. You are never alone, not even in your darkest grief.

When God told His friend, "I will go down to Egypt with you, and I will surely bring you back again," He was saying a lot more. He was saying, "Jacob, you were not alone when you thought your son was dead. You were not alone in your paralyzing sorrow. I was with you in it. And you will not be alone on the long, perilous journey to Egypt. I will be with you as you travel, and I will bring you safely home again."

Above all, God was reassuring this worn, old man that the empty void in his heart would be filled. God loved Jacob far too much to let him live alone. And He loved him too much to let him die alone. " 'And Joseph's own hand will close your eyes' " (Genesis 46:4).

When I worked as a chaplain, I would often find terminally ill patients who had managed to come to terms with the prospect of their death. They knew the end was near. But there was one thing they could not face, and that was the thought of dying alone. That was just too much.

It's for this reason that many hospitalized patients choose hospice. They want to die at home surrounded by those they know and love. As a hospital chaplain I often noticed that families would take great pains to make sure that at least one family member was always present when a loved one faced death. No one wants Mom or Dad to die alone.

One night, quite late, I got a call from a hospital. A patient in the intensive care unit (ICU) was at the point of death. When I arrived, I noticed the patient's family wasn't present. Soon afterward they called on a cell phone to tell us a bridge near their home had washed out. They were going to have to take a longer route to the hospital.

After the call, I talked to the nurse in charge, and she told me the patient wouldn't last much longer. So I walked into the ICU cubicle and stood beside a man I'd never met. This was the daddy the people on the phone had talked about. He didn't seem at all responsive. But I took his hand and leaned in close to talk quietly to him. I told him his family was on the way because they loved him dearly and wanted so much to be with him. I spoke of Jesus and His love for this man. I told him that Christ had died for him and would raise him up at the Second Coming so that the two of them could be together for all eternity.

As I held his hand, I could feel his life and warmth slipping away. A monitor showed me the oxygen level in his blood was dangerously low. His breathing grew labored and shallow; his heart rate was weak and irregular. I stood there holding this stranger's hand and speaking words of comfort and hope to him until I heard him breathe his last. I prayed over his body and asked Jesus to take care of him until the resurrection.

Twenty minutes later the family reached the hospital. We had to tell them that Daddy had died. Then I took them into his room, and they began to weep.

His daughter sobbed, "He died alone. He died all alone."

I replied, "No, I was with him. I held his hand and told him you were on your way. I told him that you loved him and wanted to be with him. And I prayed with him. I know it isn't as good as your being here, but he wasn't alone. Jesus was here, and I was here."

I'll never forget the looks of gratitude on the faces of that family. They just didn't want Daddy to die alone.

God Almighty wanted to give His friend Jacob that reassurance. He would not be alone at the end. His beloved son Joseph would be with him at the moment of death. When Jacob breathed his last, Joseph himself would place his fingers on his father's eyelids and gently close them.

And in those words there's another promise. God was describing the scene of Jacob's death in detail. That suggested God Himself would be an intimate witness. Besides Jacob and Joseph, a third party would be present, God Himself arriving as the Comforter.

Jacob would not be alone. He would die knowing Joseph loved him. He would die knowing God loved and accepted him just as he was. And he would know that death is not really the end. It's a momentary pause before the dawn of eternity.

And so Jacob found great peace as he faced the end of his life. He called his family together and spoke a special blessing over Joseph's two sons. Then he gave special directions regarding his burial. He was ready. It was time. "When Jacob had finished giving instructions to his sons, he drew his feet up into the bed, breathed his last and was gathered to his people. Joseph threw himself upon his father and wept over him and kissed him" (Genesis 49:33–50:1).

It happened just as God said it would. Joseph was there, able to close his father's eyes. And since God's spoken promise was fulfilled, we can rest assured His unspoken promise was fulfilled as well. God Almighty hovered over that deathbed. Jacob did not die alone.

No friend of God ever dies alone. I have been present at hundreds of death-bed scenes and have come to realize that people die in very different ways. Basically, we die the same way we have lived. If we live in fear, we die afraid. If we live with guilt, we die guilty. If we haven't found our way to God, we die restlessly.

But I have never seen a believer in Christ die alone. I have seen them die with courage and confidence. I have seen them die knowing they are loved and accepted. I have seen them die with an expression on their face that says they will awaken to spend eternity with their Savior. He is the One they have lived with day by day.

A lonely God loves you enough to spend every day with you. He's close by even when you don't feel His presence. He's trying to guide and teach you even when you have a hard time listening. A lonely God wants to stand by your side through thick and thin to the very end, to the moment when He leans in and gives you a comforting assurance that you will spend eternity with Him.

And that means, of course, that this lonely God loves you too much to leave you in the grave. We get hints of that in the Old Testament. And in the New Testament the "blessed hope" becomes a major theme. The life, death, and resurrection of Jesus Christ gives a whole new meaning to the phrase "life beyond the grave." It fills that hazy picture with vivid colors.

Jesus Christ stands first and foremost among many of His family members who will experience a resurrection. His promise of a second coming gives every believer a firm starting point for eternity.

It all fits into the big picture. It's all an authentic story from beginning to end. A lonely God had such a heart of love that He could not bear to live alone and without love.

So He made creatures who were capable of loving Him. But genuine love can come only from free choice. And free choice implies the capacity to reject a lover. Love is the opposite of force and coercion.

God lovingly created creatures capable of rejecting love. And when they did, His lonely heart demanded that He provide a means of reconciliation. God laid out His plan of redemption to fallen human beings. And what's more, He found countless ways to help people connect with that plan. He used any number of methods to lead them gently into spiritual intimacy with Himself.

And now that our reconciliation has been made complete through Jesus, God is pressing on toward that ultimate reunion. It breaks His heart every time He witnesses the death of one of His friends. It's hard to bear the separation. But what's really unbearable is the thought of spending eternity without us.

That's why He has promised over and over to come again. He will raise to life those who have died trusting in Christ for their reconciliation. Jesus wanted us to rest assured of that "blessed hope." So He told His disciples, " 'Do not let your hearts be troubled. Trust in God, trust also in me. In my Father's house are many rooms; if it were not so, I would have told you. I am going there to prepare a place for you. . . . I will come back and take you to be with me that you also may be where I am' " (John 14:1–3).

The One who came down from heaven told us exactly what to expect up in heaven. And what we can expect is this: intimacy in a glorious setting. Jesus wants us to be where He is. And He has determined to leave no believer behind. No matter what happens to our bodies in this life, no matter what kind of death we experience, He will raise us up to eternal life as whole individuals, just as He emerged from the tomb gloriously whole. The apostle Paul tells us exactly when and how that will happen:

> Brothers, we do not want you to be ignorant about those who fall asleep, or to grieve like the rest of men, who have no hope. We believe that Jesus died and rose again and so we believe that God will bring with Jesus those who have fallen asleep in him. According to the Lord's own word, we tell you that we who are still alive, who are left till the coming of the Lord, will certainly not precede those who have fallen asleep. For the Lord himself will come down from heaven, with a loud command, with the voice of the archangel and with the trumpet call of God, and the dead in Christ will rise first. After that, we who are still alive and are left will be caught up together with them in the clouds to meet the Lord in the air. And so we will be with the Lord forever. Therefore encourage each other with these words (1 Thessalonians 4:13–18).

A glorious resurrection is coming. It happens at Christ's second coming. And notice that the reason for the Second Coming and the reason for the resurrection are the same. In John 14, Jesus tells us that He is coming back to get us so " 'that you also may be where I am' " (verse 3). And in 1 Thessalonians 4 we are told that the reason for the resurrection is so that "we will be with the Lord forever" (verse 17).

That's the bottom line. A lonely God wants to be with us! That's why He's coming to get us. And it doesn't matter whether we are dead or alive; it doesn't matter if nothing physical remains of our lives. God has our identity, our spirit, in the palm of His hand. And He will re-create us, just as He once created Adam and Eve. He is going to take us home with Him so that we can always be with Him.

Being with Jesus is what makes heaven heaven. And the marvelous thing is this: It's our being there that makes heaven heaven for Him, too!

On the morning of August 16, 1945, a small boy ran through Shantung internment camp, shouting that he'd spotted a plane in the sky. The ragged, starving group of civilians, who'd been imprisoned by the Japanese in that compound, stumbled out to an open field, looking up at the clouds. And there it was, looking like a sea gull, approaching them from the western mountains.

As the plane came steadily nearer, the internees realized it might be coming for *them*. An electric current seemed to shoot through the waiting crowd.

Someone shouted, "Why, it's a *big* plane, with four engines!"

Another cried out, "Look, how low it is. It's almost touching the trees!"

As the hum of the aircraft grew louder, still another yelled, "Look, there's the *American flag* painted on the side!"

And then in an unbelieving daze, voices cried out, "Look, they're *waving* at us! They know who we are. They've come to get us."

At this point the excitement was more than these brutalized, homesick survivors could contain. Pandemonium broke loose. People were running in circles, shouting at the top of their lungs, waving their arms. Dignified folk were embracing people they hardly knew. Very proper English men and women were weeping. Others laughed hysterically or cried like babies.

Writer Langdon Gilkey, who was among that crowd, recalled his feelings: "This plane was *our* plane. It was sent here for *us*, to tell us the war was over. It was . . . [a] personal touch, the assurance that we were again included in the wider world."

Suddenly all the shouting stopped. The entire group gasped and stared. The underside of the plane was opening. Men were jumping out of it and floating down in parachutes. This seemed too much to believe. Their rescuers weren't just coming someday; they were coming today, *now,* to be in their midst!

This realization exploded like a bomb in the crowd, and all began running toward the compound gate. No one paused to think of the danger of armed guards and machine guns pointed down at them from the towers. Two and a half years of frustration and loneliness and pain turned into a human avalanche. It poured down the main road, hit the front gate, and burst it open. Bewildered guards just stared.

The running, yelling, ecstatic flood of humanity poured past a neighboring Chinese village and out toward a cornfield. The paratroopers were landing there. Coming up to them, Gilkey remembers, the soldiers looked almost godlike—tall, healthy, energetic. After all, they'd come from the clouds to save them.

Soon that flood of humanity, carrying the paratroopers on its shoulders, celebrating wildly, poured back to camp, through the gates, and up to the Japanese commander's quarters. He and the other guards surrendered without a fight. The war was indeed over. Freedom had come. The world was brand new again.

I do not know when, but one day soon, when a lonely God's heart is just about to burst from all the pain and loneliness, when that lonely God cannot stand the pain of separation one day longer, the sky will tear apart from one horizon to another. And we will experience an incredible rescue from the prison house of sin that this earth has become. A glorious light will shine down and illuminate the entire globe at once. That light will be brighter than a thousand suns, so bright that it will destroy the eyes of all who hate righteousness. But the light will be a welcome sight for all who love Christ. Its warmth will warm our souls. Its brightness will drive away the dark clouds of grief and guilt and sin and pain.

The entire earth will shake with excitement. Mountains will topple; islands will sink; tidal waves will roll. The heavens will be filled with thousands upon thousands of angels singing songs of glory and praise to their King. Their voices will amplify into a sublime kind of music that no human ear has ever heard.

At that moment we will know that our long night of suffering and sorrow has disappeared. The long horror story of man's cruelty to man has finally ceased. The weary, lonely struggle in a world dominated by sin is over.

There will be jubilation on the day of His coming. There will be shouts of joy as we finally realize our hope: "He's coming close; I can see the angels blowing their trumpets." The sound gets louder, the cloud of glory brighter. And we realize "He sees me. He knows who I am. He's coming to get me."

And we'll be right. Because at that moment, Jesus, our lonely Savior, will clear His voice. He is about to say something that must be heard the world over. Suddenly the most melodic, yet powerful, voice the world has ever heard cries out, "Awake, awake, awake, all you who sleep in the dust!"

The words have scarcely left His lips when the ground begins to explode in every cemetery around the world. Dirt, rock, and concrete vaults blow apart. God's friends are coming out. The ones He has missed for so long are rising from their graves with glorious new bodies.

The millions whom a lonely God has grieved over are coming out of the ground at last. Adam, Eve, Noah, Abraham, Isaac, Jacob, Joseph—they're blinking in the dazzling light. Your family and friends are looking around to get their bearings in this new world. That day witnesses overwhelming embraces, unimaginably intense reunions.

And then all rise up in the air together, every gaze fixed on Christ who seems to fill the heavens with His glory. All are headed for the rendezvous of the ages.

It's a rendezvous that God's lonely heart planned in ages past. He devised a plan to bring you safe into His arms for all eternity. Hell itself was not going to stand in the way. He would find a path around it—by laying down His own body.

We'll feel like running and shouting and waving our arms. We'll become a flood of humanity lifted up toward the Son of God. We'll know with indescribable joy that this is our God; He's coming for us—not someday, but right now, today!

Countless people in immortal bodies will gather around Him like a cloud.

We, the objects of His affection, are now the companions of His delight. He will wipe every tear from our eyes. He will fill every lonely void in our hearts.

That's the climax of the story. In heaven, and then on an earth made new, we will experience uninterrupted fellowship, face-to-face intimacy, immeasurable love forever. From that day forward, our God will be lonely no more! The final chapter of His journal will have been written. And I can imagine the last entry will be something like this: "Together at last. All My friends and I will never be lonely again!"

It's true. A lonely God loves you too much to let you live alone, too much to let you die alone, and too much to leave you in the grave alone!

How should we respond to such love? How should we respond to all the ways this lonely God has tried to woo us?

How about accepting Him into your heart today? How about deciding to live with Him every day? How about determining to be ready to welcome Him when He returns to take you home?

God wants to be with you always. That's the happy ending to the story. And we can choose it for ourselves. We can say, "Yes, Lord! I *will* be with You always. I promise, by Your grace, to spend eternity with You so that neither of us will ever be lonely again!"